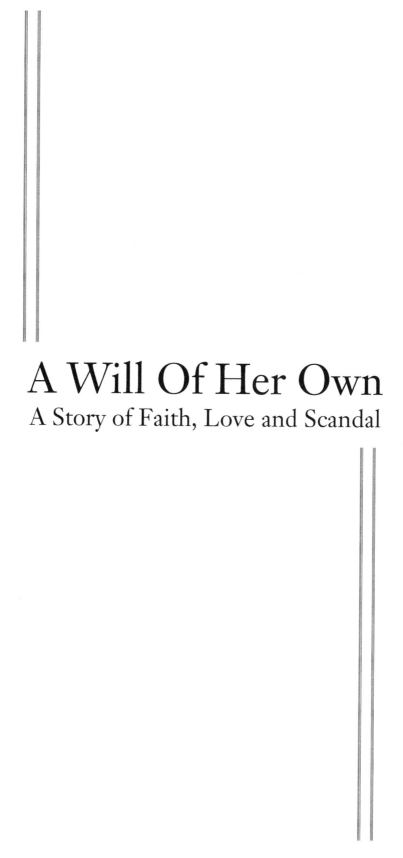

A Will Of Her Own

A Story of Faith, Love and Scandal

SHIRES PRESS
4869 Main Street
P.O. Box 2200
Manchester Center, VT 05255
www.northshire.com

A Will Of Her Own
A Story of Faith, Love and Scandal

ISBN Number: 978-1-60571-296-3
Library of Congress Number: 2016931249

Building Community, One Book at a Time
A family-owned, independent bookstore in
Manchester Ctr., VT, since 1976 and Saratoga Springs, NY since 2013.
We are committed to excellence in bookselling.
The Northshire Bookstore's mission is to serve as a resource for information,
ideas, and entertainment while honoring the needs of customers,
staff, and community.

Printed in the United States of America

Cover photo by Christian Hoffman
Author photo by Mark McCarty

A Will Of Her Own
A Story of Faith, Love and Scandal

Mary Scanlan

For Maura and Kira

How many loved your moments of glad grace
And loved your beauty with love false or true
But one man loved the pilgrim soul in you
And loved the sorrows of your changing face.

When You Are Old
W.B. Yeats

CONTENTS

LOVE

SCANDAL

PROLOGUE

For decades I have wanted to write this story, but I didn't do so because of shame, guilt, unresolved anger, fear of retribution and an excessive sense of privacy and personal integrity.

In 1968 Will and I were dinner guests at the home of an esteemed faculty member of the university where Will was working. Newly married and new to the community, we had not told our courtship tale to anyone except the dean and his staff when they interviewed Will, lest he be treated like a curiosity – and our marriage treated like a scandal. But even though we requested confidentiality about our circumstances from the dean, word seeped out in this small town that Will had been a priest and I was his "girl from New York."

In preparation for my debut at the dinner, I changed my outfit three times, crying fearfully about meeting people in this new world whom I thought were much more important, and probably much more intelligent than I.

We arrived late but only by a few minutes and were warmly greeted by our hosts, the dean and his wife. I was impressed with the modern art adorning the walls and the rows of bookcases comfortably at home in each room. When we were all summoned to the dinner table, I was seated opposite a terribly self-important middle-aged historian. Somewhere between the main course and the salad, and after a few glasses of wine, he loudly addressed me: "So what brought you two together?" Unable to ignore his leering smile, realizing that he knew, or thought he knew our story, and flushing with embarrassment and annoyance, I responded, "Sex." I don't know where that retort came from, but I loved it, loved deflating the loudmouth's taunt. The entire table went silent until Will and I started laughing. I gave them the answer they wanted, without any details.

But it wasn't a true answer.

I began writing "A Will of Her Own" to tell the story to our daughters. For too long, they had been told snippets of tales about their father and me whenever an issue or the occasion demanded it. I thought I was writing a simple little memoir to set the record straight. However, as my story developed, my writing shifted. No longer would a brief personal account of their parents' love suffice. I needed to tell my daughters the story of moving from the religion of my youth to faith, and growing from and learning about sex and romance to learning about love.

FAITH

About a Catholic Girlhood

MORNING PRAYERS

By the time I was ten, I knew how I wanted to start my day. I negotiated my morning routine with my parents who gave their approval because they knew my destination. Slipping out of bed, I washed up, put on my plaid uniform jumper, white blouse, socks and ugly brown shoes and headed out, careful not to bang the door.

The streets, which would soon be bustling, were empty except, I thought, for me. I skipped, marched, slouched and zigzagged around cracks in the sidewalk, singing whatever song was in my head. Nobody told me, "Keep your shoulders back." The light from the sky was so pure and friendly. I was on a mission. I was on my way to church.

It was the 1950s. We lived in a brick two-family house in Sunnyside, Queens. We were six – Mother and Dad and the four of us children – living in the whole house, four bedrooms and two bathrooms. The place felt full but never cramped, even when we were eight for the years when both grandmothers came to live and die with us, and sometimes more than that when a struggling cousin came for respite or an uncle or aunt stayed for an extended visit.

Sunnyside was one of the first suburbs in Queens, developed in the early 20th century with the completion of the 59th Street Bridge spanning the East River from Manhattan. In the 1920s, my father and grandmother saw it as an investment opportunity. Dad relished his daily bus ride to and from Sunnyside, not caring how long the commuting took because he enjoyed the sights and sounds of Manhattan, his beloved hometown.

My father, Bartholomew, was born in 1902 in New York City, the son of an Irish-immigrant mother and a first-generation Irish-American father. His paternal grandfather, David, who had emigrated in 1857, was a doorman on Manhattan's Upper East Side.

The doorman's son, James, my father's father, was the franchise owner of a bar on 37th Street and Third Avenue, and his family lived in an apartment above it. The story of how he died is not very well known in my family. But the story I know is that when my father was three years old, his father died of a ruptured appendix. At first, his widow took in laundry to support herself, her son and younger daughter. She then moved her family to a tenement on the Upper East Side, working on the cooking staff for a wealthy family and later becoming a live-in servant chef. When he reached the age of twelve, my father was sent to live with another family as a "liver-in," meaning he lived there for room and board. He visited his mother and sister regularly, but the separation from them – and being fatherless – made him feel abandoned, not by any malice, but by circumstances, which led him to refer to himself later in life as an orphan. The Catholic Church and especially the Christian Brothers were his extended family.

In Sunnyside, it was four-block walk past brick homes with small gardens and a few apartment buildings along the tree-lined streets to our parish church, St. Teresa The Little Flower of Jesus. The church at that time was in the basement of my school. It had no spire. The sanctuary was just a box with pews and kneelers. There were statues and confessionals. The altar was plain. But the room was dark and cozy and comforting in its tightness and the smell of candle wax and incense.

My mission was the 6:30 a.m. Mass, but not just the service. I wanted to be with myself and with my God and the Blessed Mother.

I prayed to whichever saint I needed to solve a problem: "St. Joseph, patron saint of the dying, help my grandmother. St. Jude, patron saint of the impossible, help me love my brother. St. Anthony, help me find my gold locket. All ye saints in heaven help me with my dirty and lustful thoughts. Tell me that I'm all right, tell me that I'm normal, tell me that I can do whatever I need to this day. Help me to love, help me to be a good girl. Help me to find someone who will love me later on when I'm older."

It wasn't a prayer of desperation. I was too young for that. It was a prayer of supplication and honor to those who had made it in glory through life, made it to heaven and weren't being tormented in purgatory or hell. The virgin martyrs went to heaven after rape and torture and social disgrace. I thought they were wonderful. I was comforted in the ritual of the Mass and convinced it would help me through the day. I couldn't possibly have understood much of the service. It was in Latin. But it had a familiar rhythm, familiar patterns. We gave glory. We admitted our failings. We triumphed through the church.

That hour gave me assurance of my independence. I rejected anyone who asked to join me. "Thanks," I'd say, "but I'd rather be alone." On my walk home, I felt the strength and calm I needed for the must-have breakfast, the line for the bathroom and the last-minute search for books and papers.

This was the heyday of the Catholic Church in New York City and its growing suburbs. The Brooklyn Diocese, which included Brooklyn, Queens and Long Island, was huge. When I was a teenager, our parish held a fund drive and built a large new church of white stone with massive Romanesque arches. It had mahogany pews, ornate marble statues and a mural of Jesus, triumphant in heaven, arms extended, embracing the world. I found a pew off to the side in that ornate building so that I could still feel the comfort of the little old church.

FINDING OUR ROOTS

My mother came from a large Irish-American family who lived in the coal region of Pennsylvania. Born Alice McDonald in 1903, she was the second of eight siblings. Three died of illnesses that destroyed young children in the early part of the 20th century.

She would become a beloved high school English teacher in her hometown of Girardville, so popular that her students published a farewell tribute to Miss McDonald when she went off to marry the dashing Bart Sheehan from Manhattan. She kept the tribute in her file of special papers all her life. The students' letter began:

"Alice C. McDonald graduated from GHS in 1920. She was a student at Keystone State Normal School, Kutztown, Pa., 1920-22. She studied Junior High work at Susquehanna University and received her A.B. in 1928. She taught in the grade schools of the Girardville Borough for four years, and was English instructress in Girardville High School for six years."

The tribute went on to praise her "poise, dignity, a keen sense of humor and, best of all, understanding." Her students said she "could make even the most restless boys sit up and listen to her reading poetry."

After their wedding in St. Joseph's Church, decorated from altar to altar with lilies from her father's garden, Mother moved into her husband's home in Queens. She traded the prominent social position her Edwardian family enjoyed in the coal-mining town for anonymity in a burgeoning suburb. At first, she knew no one but her mother-in-law, and her sister-in-law and her family, who, with the young couple, shared the two-family house. My father traveled a lot in his work for Arthur Andersen, the pre-eminent accounting firm of that time, and then his work with the Treasury Department sent him traveling throughout Europe. She missed him greatly, but when her husband came home from work, he greeted his mother in her section of the house first and then greeted his wife.

After eight years of marriage, I was born. Mother was thrilled. Dad was ecstatic. The rest of the family was happy my parents finally had a child. My sister was born one year, one month and one day later, followed by our brother two years, one month and four days after that and then our youngest sister eleven months and twenty-one days later. We took over the whole house.

"I'm putting all of our dentist's kids through college," Dad always said when he was paying the dental bills.

"It runs in the family," they said. "Too much sugar," they said.

"Not enough brushing," they said.

But the fact is we all had cavities in those days before fluoride and flossing.

We had been going to Dr. Keneally since we started school. One of us seemed to be in the chair every few months. His office on 44th Street and 50th Avenue was right across from our church, in the same building as our family doctor. He was the good Catholic dentist of our neighborhood. To my mother and father, the site of his office near the church added to his credentials. His profile fit my family's criteria for the acceptable good guy – tall and handsome with sandy hair, chiseled features, muscular. He could have played football in college. He had seven children.

With my parents, he was charming and professional. However, no parent was ever allowed into the room when a child was in the chair. "You'll only get in the way and may upset your kid," he told parents. So I went alone to his office with instructions to be a good girl and do as I was told.

The waiting room was always filled. The dentist was always late. I read the outdated, finger-worn magazines, waiting nervously on the brown plastic chairs for the nurse to summon me. When I entered his room he smiled at me. I climbed into the chair and tried to recline, my body rigid, shoulders crunched up to my ears, hands clenched on my lap, legs crossed and locked at the ankle. I can't remember a nurse or an assistant ever in the room. Good humor quickly left the scene once the exam began.

"Stop fidgeting!" he said, boring the drill deeper into one of the back teeth of my adolescent mouth. My cheek burned. My eyes smarted. Usually, in order to get my submission, he just pressed his massive hand on my shoulder. This time he seemed unusually irritated and impatient. I wasn't sure what I was doing wrong, but I didn't dare ask. I devised all kinds of excuses to myself for his mean and punishing behavior. He's tired. My mouth is too small for his hands. It's late in the day. He has a lot on his mind. It's all my fault. I still associate the odor of antiseptic mouthwash and overworked dental equipment with danger.

Dentists, doctors, teachers, priests, nuns, parents, anyone older, grownups I didn't even know–all were treated as revered authorities to be obeyed without questioning.

"Not that we are inferior in any way, mind you," Mother would proclaim in her most haughty voice, dragging out our pedigree. But adults, especially professionals, were never to be questioned. I wondered then why some of Dad's clients would argue with him when he worked with them in our house. After all, he was a professional.

Mother loved managing her home and her little tribe of three redheads and one brunette. There was always a crowd of relatives and friends in our home, lots of laughter and talk, lots of music, but little intimacy. I don't remember ever playing with Mother alone. I do remember her reading to us, playing the piano when the family got together every Sunday, laughing with her husband over his silly jokes.

When we were school children, we traveled for a week or so each summer piled in our family station wagon. Mother enjoyed traveling, not because it was fun but because it was an educational adventure for us. She also loved reading, and any kind of musical or theatrical performance brought her pleasure. We each "played" a musical instrument, and we wrote plays together for family entertainment, but there was never a moment I remember snuggling with her in a chair.

She was competent, we were obedient; she was stern, we were compliant. Dad was boisterous, funny and affectionate. She was proper, quiet spoken, withholding in affection. Her idea of a kiss was to turn her face to the side of your lips to permit you to plant a kiss on her high-boned cheek.

Vestiges of "children should be seen but not heard" colored the child-rearing standards of our home. At family parties, we could be more free, although even in the midst of childhood play, Grandma could be counted on to admonish us that "laughing comes to crying" if we were too raucous.

Performing for our elders was done without questioning, with one exception – my little sister Ann, the last of the brood of first cousins. When it was her turn to perform, she had a crying act that always won the heart of all the parents, aunts and uncles. "Ah, let her be. She's just a baby," they said to the great annoyance of the rest of us who had already sung our song, danced our hornpipe, played our piano or violin solo.

Performance, perfection, pleasing. Failure to meet those expectations was an implied moral failing. Being a good girl was the game I learned to play, and I played it personally and professionally for a long time, inhibiting my maturation and leading to later physical and emotional anguish.

I knew that if I disobeyed the dentist, my parents would hear about it. I knew what happened to Jim when he had trouble with the nuns in school. "Go home and tell your parents what bad things your brother did in school today," the third-grade teacher, Sister Catherine Eugene, told me one day, ticking off his supposed misdemeanors. I was so upset that I told my parents only after I said it was "not fair, but she made me tell on him." His punishment was loud and strong and humiliating.

I learned cunning and deceitfulness, politeness and perfectionism. I was an expert at meeting adult expectations. I also learned how to meet my own needs when they conflicted with Mother and Dad. I learned how to keep secrets, to covertly get what I wanted when it was important to me, to devise elaborate plots to meet with friends who weren't on the approved list and to deal with parental wrath when I confessed my secret or got caught. I learned fear of authority.

I began to grow up when I became a spiritual and intellectual rebel. When I was in high school, rebellion meant staying out past curfew, meeting friends in the forbidden candy store and riding in cars. I experimented with smoking cigarettes while standing on the first-floor toilet and blowing the smoke out the bathroom window to disguise the smell of tobacco.

One night my father collected me at the candy store where all my friends hung out. For some reason, I was forbidden to go there. Oh the humiliation as I suddenly saw him charging up the street, red faced and bellowing, "Mary, get over here!"

"Oh Lord, I gotta go," I sheepishly murmured to my friends, slinking away and wanting to murder my father.

I was almost cured of ignoring curfews when I was a senior in high school. "Be home by 11," Dad told me as I headed out to a party.

"No one else has to go home until 1," I retorted. "That's when I'll be home."

"Eleven is it!" he yelled back.

I came home around 1:00 in the morning, when I said I would, to find my father and two policemen waiting for me in the living room. My father had notified the police that I was missing. Oh the humiliation! After the officers left, Dad and I had a bitter argument and remained silent with each other for the rest of the weekend. He won. I won. No one won. Both of our wills took a beating that night.

NUNS I HAVE KNOWN

I always knew when one of them was near. They smelled so good. It was the smell of soap and starch, never perfume. No matter how old they were – and no one ever knew that fact– the Dominican sisters at my elementary school seemed to float off the ground as they walked. I thought they went around on gliders of some kind. Except for Sister John Marie, my fifth-grade teacher. She was a tomboy in nun's clothing. She never walked up the staircase. She bounded up two steps at a time, while yelling at us to "walk like ladies."

Faces and hands were the only visible parts of the nuns' bodies. Everything else was swathed in heavy ivory-colored cotton cloth. Beneath their wide long sleeves was another wrist-tight sleeve where handkerchiefs were discretely tucked. Black serge veils flowed from starched, shoulder-length white linen facial coifs, all kept on the crown or their heads by large hatpins. Their floor-length dresses were belted loosely with black leather that held rosaries and keys. They rustled and jangled as they swished around, long skirts rubbing against heavy black stockings.

Their individuality peeked out in the vague outlines of their bodies – tall and short, round and skinny, generous sagging bosoms or no discernable breasts – and in the shape and size of their low-heeled black brogue shoes. Unless they were bowed by age (and maybe too many years of being bowed in prayer), their posture was perfect. They stood in church and in the school hallway or playground with arms folded somewhat menacingly in their long scapulars. The pretty ones glowed in the starched coifs that tightly outlined their faces. The facial binds also exaggerated the sagging features of those who were homely and overweight.

School started at 9 a.m. We little girl cherubs in our plaid jumpers, white shirts and brown shoes and boys in white shirts, navy blue jackets, ties and trousers stood and stared at the crucifix on the wall over the desk in front of the classroom. "In the name of the Father, and of the Son, and of the Holy Ghost," we said following with a "Hail Mary" and an "Our Father." The day ended at 3 p.m. with the same prayers. The trick was not to catch anyone's eye during this solemn time so that you wouldn't start giggling.

When I was in the second grade at St. Teresa's, I began taking piano lessons after school, in the convent. I'd bashfully enter the building and head to the music room, eyes cast down to the oriental rugs decorating the polished floors in the hallways and parlors. I'd pass the large kitchen where meals were prepared for the sisters. It always smelled so good. One day, I furtively looked to see what was going on. Nothing exciting or interesting, as a matter of fact. The cook was cooking!

The first floor was open to the public. Only special people were admitted to the second floor where the fifteen nuns slept, each in a simple cell-like room. By the time I was in eighth grade, after five years of weekly lessons in the convent, I was deemed mature enough to be admitted to the second floor. "Go tell Sister Catherine Eugene she has a visitor," one of the nuns instructed me one day while I was waiting for my lesson. That meant quietly climbing the wide, carpeted staircase to the endless second-floor corridor and finding the room with Sister's name on the door's nameplate. My heart fluttered with excitement for this special assignment. I gingerly knocked on Sister's door and announced her waiting visitor. She casually opened her door, and I saw the sight I was hoping for. She was veil-less! I noticed nothing but her white coif before she turned and pinned on her black veil. I always hoped that some hair would peek out from under their coifs. For some reason, seeing hair would mean they were mere women, mere mortals. "Wonder if any of them are redheads," I dreamily mused.

The first-floor music room featured an upright spinet piano, always with sparkling clean keys and perfectly in tune. On the wall above the piano, St. Cecilia, surrounded by red roses cascading from heaven, gazed down at me from a dark gilt-framed painting. A virgin martyr and the patron saint of music, she was to be my music model. My teacher, Sister Gabriella, with her constant slight cough, was in love with her God and never seemed happy, but she was never mean. In spite of her wan, passive demeanor, she was an excellent piano teacher. She guided me for many years before finally passing me on to a more advanced teacher. When I left Sister Gabriella's care, I worried about her future. She was probably in her thirties when I knew her, but she was so pale and thin that I thought she was close to death. "She's like the virgin saints," I told my friend Alberta.

Sister Petronella, the principal of our school, was a crotchety old Irish woman. She ruled with a gruff exterior and a generous heart. For some reason, she loved redheads, so I was a favored student. When I was in the fifth grade, I was given the chance to help one of the parish priests, Father Dermody, run the mimeograph machine each week. We would meet in the school library on Fridays and run off hundreds of pages on a messy, inky machine. This was probably the church bulletin for the upcoming Sunday. We never discussed the contents. He was a gentle and funny man whom I learned to trust – or so I thought then.

Sister Mary Raymond, my small, dark fifth-grade homeroom teacher, was from the Philippines, had a heavy accent and spit when she spoke. She drilled us in Palmer Method handwriting exercises for an hour after lunch every day. Not only did I master penmanship that year, I also learned about corporal punishment.

The boys had a particularly difficult time with the Palmer Method. Writing pages of letters over and over again with a perfect slant and oval was not their idea of an hour of fun or education. One of them, the shortest boy in the class, tormented Sister, imitating her as she spat her words out. Of course, she caught him and, of course, she punished him.

"Francis DeFeo," she bellowed. "Come with me now." She then led him to the back of the classroom, into the dark cloakroom, which stretched across the back of the room, and hung him on one of the hooks by his jacket collar. We were all titillated but afraid to laugh out loud for fear of joining Francis in that closet where, for the entire year, he spent at least one day a week hanging by the back of his jacket collar. I always wondered if he was permanently damaged by that torture, although he took it in stride.

I was an obedient girl and frightened by the sadistic beatings boys received when they misbehaved, especially when the nuns hit them on the back of their bare knees with a steel ruler. Hearing the command from Sister, "Go to the library and roll up your trousers," meant punishment was on its way. No matter which room we were in, we always seemed to be able to hear the bellowing. This was one way these women maintained control in classrooms with more than more than seventy children. There was no such thing as teacher assistants in our school.

And, we left our homeroom once a week for music, elocution and art instruction. Every other subject was covered in that homeroom without any other adult supervision. There was neither gym nor organized physical education. We just played in the separate playgrounds during the afternoon recess – boys on one side of the building, girls on the other.

During the six years I attended the parish school, I was always in competition with Thomas Smith, the brightest boy in the class. "Whadidya get?" he would hiss at me as we lined up in the church to receive our report cards from the pastor. I had a huge crush on him and hated to tell him the truth. True, I wanted to be first, but even more I wanted him to like me. It was in that dark and narrow hallway coming out of the church where Tommy always got me. He demanded an accounting, and we would compare 96.5 to 96.4 averages, or something of that order. It killed him when I, a girl, beat him. "You think you're so smart, don't you? You're just lucky, Red," he said, calling me by the nickname I hated. I loved him in spite of it.

Of course the nuns encouraged competition. And although I couldn't document it, I believe that, with special energy, they wanted the girls to succeed. At the very least, the girls were easier to control on a day-to-day basis in those overcrowded rooms where those virginal women used the power of the habit to manage overstimulated, repressed young Catholics.

Bless Me, Father

Secrets are a wondrous thing. They can be an adrenalin rush, full of glamour, danger, uncertainty and power. They can be exhausting, undermine confidence, strain relationships and ultimately fly in the face of my values. Secrets build trust and destroy it. Secrets are sensual and demeaning. Secrets are powerful and crippling. Secrets can ruin friendships, create shaky alliances, mask imperfections. Secrets are top secret, in secret, the veil of secrecy, the oath of secrecy, deep secret, secret ink, family secrets, keeping secret, the seal of secrecy, in secret, secret meetings, secret passages, the secret to success, trade secrets, secret loves, secret lives, secrets of the deep sea.

I learned about secrets when I was seven years old and in training for my First Confession, in preparation for my First Holy Communion. Sister Margaret, my second-grade teacher, joyfully spent the year giving us special instruction on the rituals of both sacraments. We practiced walking demurely with our hands folded in prayer position at our hearts, genuflecting while keeping our backs straight and not tumbling over, remembering the words to spill out when the confessional door was slid open.

We practiced tipping our heads back just so when the priest reached us at the Communion railing and gave us the host while we kept our eyes closed and put our tongues out just far enough to catch the dry unleavened bread. Most importantly, we learned not to chew Jesus, the dry host, but to let it dissolve on our tongues and slip down our throats. All this was drilled into us until the May Day when we went to the church for our practice First Confession with the priest. I was finally in the big wood confessional box. It was a scary place, dark and mysterious despite Sister's attempts to enlighten us. I really didn't know what a priest was, although I knew he was one of the most important people in the world, according to Mother and Dad and all the nuns. And he had, we were told, the Seal of the Confessional, a magical trick incomprehensible to a seven-year-old.

I made my First Communion with my class, all eighty-one of us, resplendent in my faux white bridal dress, veil, white stockings and shoes, and itchy white lace gloves. My hair was in long red curls, the braids loosened for this special occasion. Someone, maybe my parents, gave me a white silk-covered prayer book, which I still have, and crystal rosary beads. I felt really special. But my deepest memory of the day is my cousin Rhoda pinching me on the back of my arm during our family party, just to be sure I remembered that I wasn't hot stuff, that she was an elder cousin.

For the next few years of elementary school, I practiced my confession during our Saturday afternoon walk to church. The family rule was that we all had to go to confession each week in preparation for Sunday Mass and Communion. It was as routine as the Saturday night bath. We all knew that if we had committed a mortal sin, we had to confess in order to receive Communion at Mass. If you didn't go to Communion, everyone knew that you "were in mortal sin." By the time I was a teenager, absence at Communion was always interpreted by our friends as an indication of some forbidden sexual fun the week before.

I was convinced that the priest in the confessional box would remember me from the previous week and know that I was the girl who had confessed anger with my brother or swear words or disobedience, as well as the number of times I had committed these offenses. My trick, which my young girl brain thought was unique, was to change the content and quantity of my sins each week. My confessional content had to do with authority, schoolgirl pranks, jealousies and untruths. There was no spirituality to it, no therapeutic effect, nor did I expect spiritual advice or therapy. I expected only to be forgiven my sins by the priest who represented God and to be returned to what was called a state of grace. State of grace – to my young mind – meant something like the State of New York. I thought that the nuns meant that your soul was cleansed white when you were in a state of grace, gray when you had venial sins and black when you committed mortal sin. At least that's what Sister Margaret showed us with those analytical drawings on the second-grade blackboard showing an egg-shaped thing filled in totally in white chalk, partially shaded or, worst of all, no chalk at all, all black except for the outline of the egg.

The confession line was longest for the gentlest confessor. Sometimes the pastor swept through the church, moving us to shorter lines and more stern confessors. I carefully avoided eye contact with anyone, not wanting to see them, not wanting them to see me in my state of sin. When the green light went on over the middle door of the confessional, it was safe to enter. Kneeling in the dark box, waiting for the screen to slide open, I strained to hear which priest was in there, trying to guess his mood by the tone of his muffled voice before he opened the screen to my side. "Bless me, Father, for I have sinned. It has been one week since my last confession." "Yes, my daughter, go ahead." "I disobeyed my father, I got angry at my brother twice, and I said bad words five times." Those were the early days of rehearsed confessions. I monitored my language and tried to minimize the magnitude of my sin.

I plotted out each week. My confessed sins were all so petty until adolescence and the onslaught of sexual life when I found it hard to believe that the priest, a mortal man, could keep any secrets, especially luscious ones, could keep community gossip, could keep serious offenses – murder, rape, child abuse – to himself.

I reported only on what I was told was wrong. I was in the confessional to talk about being a naughty girl so that I could cleanse my soul and return to a state of grace. Any questions about sexual activity came from the priest. "Bless me, Father, for I have sinned. I was making out with my boyfriend, and we were petting." Father always replied, "Above the waist or below?" On the way to church, I prayed that question wouldn't come up, but it was inevitably part of the dialogue.

By the time I was sixteen, that box had been transformed into a place of shame and anger, still dark but no longer scary. When I was eighteen, I left it in disgust and rage. I had gone to confession, excited that I had an intellectual issue to discuss with Father Dermody, the supportive and quiet man whom I had admired since the days of the mimeograph work in the school library.

"Father," I said, "I need to read some books by Renan and Schweitzer and Strauss about the historical Jesus, for a paper I'm writing for my history class. I know they're on the Index, but I know you'll give me your permission to read them for school." "You know I can't do that," he responded. "If they're on the Index of Forbidden Books, you absolutely cannot read them."

I was furious that he would not even discuss with me the possibility of reading books for college research just because they were listed as forbidden to be read by Catholics "under pain of mortal sin." I was also mad at myself for stupidly hoping I would have a rational discussion with a priest. I left that confessional in Sunnyside never to return to another dark box smelling of cigarette smoke, alcohol, garlic, incense and the body of whomever had knelt at the screen just before me.

I lovingly remember that innocent little girl who so wanted her soul to look like a white egg. Beyond that sweet feeling, I can recall nothing positive from those eleven years of confession. I have no memory of relief or cleansing or the satisfaction of feeling good about myself when I left that smelly old box.

EDUCATION THE CATHOLIC WAY

One day, in a fit over something with the new pastor, Dad ripped us out of our elementary school in Sunnyside. I was in the seventh grade, two years from graduating with my class. We were now, all four of us, no questions asked, off to St. Stanislaus School in the unknown land of Maspeth. This Queens neighborhood was too far away to walk to, so we went there in a carpool that Mother and a couple of other moms put together, or we took a bus.

On the first day of classes, as I tried to slink in unnoticed, my heart dropped. There were no school uniforms. I had on all the wrong clothes. Mother had bribed me with a beautiful moss green sweater to match a new plaid pleated skirt. I wore green knee socks, my size 9½ feet were shod in dark brown oxfords, I looked gawky, and I was taller than all the other girls who wore perky pastel sweaters and really cute shoes. Cheeks burning, I walked with my head down and shoulders rounded, behind Sister Justa, the principal, pretending I was invisible. We were on our way to meet Sister Stephanus, the seventh-grade homeroom teacher and my new classmates.

"Class," Sister Justa said in her Irish brogue, "please greet Miss Sheehan. I want you to welcome her and be nice to her." She put me in the first seat of the first row.

"Oh Lord," I thought, not daring to look around, staring straight ahead at the blackboard.

In spite of Sister Justa's admonition, I sat alone for the first few weeks hunched over the lunch I brought from home, pretending to eat but unable to do so and ready to cry.

The first period after lunch was social studies. It turned out to be such a scary lesson that I had a stomachache the whole time. After that first day I could never eat lunch without getting that stomachache. Each night the homework assignment was to memorize pages from the New York State Regents social studies text. The following day, presiding from her desk, Sister Stephanus would start reading the first of the assigned pages and then bellow, "You! Next!" Then one of us would pick up where she left off, reciting from memory the next sentences on the page.

Around the room she went. One by one we had to recite until she decided to move on or when we fumbled our lines. The front row seat was for the student who had the text perfectly memorized. I never left that seat all year. The rest of the class played musical desks, bumped further back in the room as they flubbed that next sentence on cue. I have no idea what we learned that year. I only know I always felt sick, which I whined about to my parents, to no avail.

Soon enough, however, I moved on to my last year in that school. Becoming the darling of the nuns didn't endear me to my classmates. I never was invited to anyone's home. During those two miserable years, I never replaced my friendships at home with Rosemary Anton, Patricia Driscoll, Alberta Ciocia, Teresa Costello, Christine Kepple, Diana Barry and my best friend, Margaret Driscoll. "I feel really weird there," I confided to her. Although I prayed for forgiveness for my evil thoughts about my classmates, I couldn't wait until graduation.

When it came, eighth grade graduation day was one of sorrow for me. My classmates hated me as I walked away, to my chagrin, with the two highest academic awards. My angry and mean classmates thought these prizes were going to their friends.

"She's only been here two years," they whispered loudly enough so I could hear, sneering as we took off our caps and gowns. I couldn't wait to get away from the jealousy and backbiting, wishing that the nuns had just ignored me. I had been awarded the only full high school scholarship available to a student from our home parish. I offered it to my dear friend Patricia from my old school, St. Teresa's, who had six brothers and sisters. I wanted her to be my friend always, and I was so afraid she'd hate me for winning.

"It's yours. You deserve it," she assured me. "You scored a perfect 100. I only got a 95." We tearfully hugged and promised to be friends forever. She went on to a prestigious private Catholic girl's school on a scholarship.

I was nervous about Bishop McDonnell Memorial High School, knowing it was super competitive. It was established in 1926 as the first Brooklyn diocesan school devoted to the education of young women, capturing the best girls from Queens and Long Island Catholic elementary schools. We were taught by five different orders of nuns – in gray stiff or flowing veils of different colors, or in little black caps, wool gowns, gray wool socks and sandals, or in floor-length ivory or black dresses. They were the elite scholars of their orders. It took us a while to figure out who was who and what her discipline was. The principal, Father Cavanaugh, was the only male in the school.

Classes in the first two years were held in an annex at a school not too far from home. I was back with five of my old friends from St. Teresa's who had all been awarded the scholarship from that parish. Since it had a larger population, St. Teresa's could award more than one scholarship each year. Classes at the annex were small and intense. The nuns were cold and smart and demanding, encouraging competition and always warning us about the potential failure of our futures if we didn't study and work hard.

We entered junior year at the main building on Eastern Parkway in the Crown Heights neighborhood of Brooklyn. In the 1950s, the neighborhood was shifting from being a posh bedroom community for Manhattan to a place of racial turbulence and tension between Hasidic Jews and African Americans and West Indian immigrants. The school was flanked by the Brooklyn Museum and the Botanical Gardens. On first sight, the building was overwhelming, a Greek Revival structure, with pillars and sweeping staircases and many, many hallways and rooms. It took weeks for me to find my way around. I seemed to always get lost on the main floor, unable to remember which of the grand staircases to use.

On good days, getting to school took an hour and a half each way riding the subway. Most times I commuted with my friends. Some days I went home alone after working in the school newspaper office. I changed trains at Grand Central, walking from one tunnel to another to catch the Flushing line, which, to my relief, traveled only for a couple of stops underground and then rose like a great cobra to the elevated lines above the industrial streets of Astoria. Dank and cold in the winter, those trains always smelled of garlic, stale cigarette smoke, booze and B.O.

Perhaps he got my attention because there were so few people around. Usually in the afternoon I was mulling over the intrigues of the school day and pretty immune to my surroundings. This day, however, I noticed a balding middle-aged man hovering in a corner of the platform on the opposite side of the tracks as I waited for my train to Queens. The smile on his pale face was a leer. His eyes, cold and gray, were staring hard at me. I scoped him out, and then I saw it. His penis was poking out of his shabby dark pants. I wasn't sure what I was seeing, never having seen an erect penis. My stomach lurched. I gagged and turned abruptly, frantically walking toward the other end of the platform. Enraged and scared, I found a spot next to an older woman and stood there until the train arrived. When I was safe inside, I looked out the window to see if the creep was still there. The platform was empty. I stopped trembling.

I told no one. For the rest of the week, I arranged to only travel with my friends after school. The following week, I rode alone once again. "I'm not going to look," I told myself, testing my courage. "And anyway, he won't be there," I continued, reassuring myself. Ever so gingerly, I forced my eyes to the platform corner. There he was. Same shabby clothes, same leer, same penis. This time I gave him what I thought was a hard, judgmental stare before darting to a small crowd further down my side of the platform. Again, he disappeared before the train left the station. Then again and again he was there, immobile and powerful in his lewd corner. I was alone and terrified. I wanted to scream at him, I wanted to tell the people around me to look at him, but after I darted away, he was nowhere to be seen.

I fretted for a month about telling my friends. I was sure they would think I was lying, making up a story to make myself look like a heroine, thinking I had a dirty mind or was just crazy. Finally, I got Patricia, Alberta and Rosemary together and told them about The Creep.

"What am I doing to make him do this to me?" I asked them. They were titillated and as scared as I was. None of them wanted to go with me to see if The Creep was there.

"You have to tell your parents," they agreed.

"Oh Lord," I said. "Dad will have a fit."

"Then don't complain to us unless you tell them," they chimed in together.

The last day I saw The Creep was no different from the first. He was standing in his corner, smiling his sickly smile, furtively pulling out his penis when he spotted me. Something in my heart changed that day. I was enraged. After dinner that night I tearfully started the conversation with my parents.

"There's this man who seems to be waiting for me every day at Grand Central and he, um, is always in a corner, and, um, he's smiling at me, and, um, he exposes himself to me. I'm sorry."

Ignoring my tears, Dad got into his best executive mode, came over to me, his face flushed with embarrassment, fear and rage. He hugged me for a long time, whispering, "It's all right. You did the right thing telling us. We'll take care of this." Then he left the room.

Mother stayed with me, silently holding my hand, as I sobbed uncontrollably. When Dad returned, he told me his friend, who was going to help me, was coming over to meet me that very evening.

I thought I knew all of Dad's friends, but I had never met this muscular, middle-aged Irishman before. He told me he was an undercover cop. "I'm just going to come to school with you for a while, Honey," he said. "We'll get that guy, don't you worry." The next day, he started traveling with me to and from school. I was hardly ever aware of him and never spoke to him. Within a couple of weeks, The Creep was arrested. I didn't see the arrest, and I didn't see him.

The day before I had to appear in court, I went to my homeroom teacher, Sister Renee, a beautiful and brilliant physicist hiding under her nun's habit. When I told her the story and that I would be absent because I had to go to court, she quietly put firm arms around me. "I'm so sorry that you have to go through this," she said softly. "You're too young for this. I'll pray for you." I cried all over her ivory habit, emptying my heart of those months of fear and rage.

I tried not to show my anxiety as I sat facing him in the courtroom. The Creep was convicted and sent to prison. I didn't understand the details and only wanted to get out of that courtroom and away from him. For a long while I feared he would get out of jail and find me. It took years for my fear of subways to lessen.

I was at the Brooklyn school for only a year when there was a major announcement from the Diocesan Education Office. For reasons unknown to us at the time, the superintendent had decided that those who were in a January graduating class would be accelerated to graduate the previous June. Instead of enjoying a year as seniors, we would be graduating in six months. We would have to double up on all our classes, beginning the day at 7 a.m. and ending at 5 p.m. There would no longer be time for modern language classes because we had to continue Latin. But of course we had to continue the boring, irrelevant religion classes where we never studied the Bible. In fact, we never even opened it. There was never a discussion about faith. Our religious education was primarily a monotonous text of "don'ts" with a smattering of church history. There were plenty of lectures about the rules of Catholicism.

At least for our last six months, there would be no phys ed classes – no more traipsing through the streets of Brooklyn in nice weather, an embarrassed flock of teenage girls in royal blue bloomer gym suits and white, white sneakers. Hooray!

Confusion about the fast-approaching graduation spread like wildfire through our class. The nuns saw the sudden deadline as an opportunity and began recruiting girls for their novitiates. Some had decided I had a vocation to become a nun because I could produce decent religious poster art. One nun, in particular, hounded me daily about joining her order, stalking me in the hallways between classes, annoying me at lunch.

On graduation morning I pulled my father aside shortly before breakfast. "Dad, Sister Patricia Clare is going to tell you I have a vocation to be a nun and that I should go to the novitiate after graduation. Please, please don't listen to her."

"Don't worry, Toots," he assured me. "I'll take care of her." And he did.

Some of my friends were vulnerable to the recruitment, which promised a college education and a lifetime of sisterhood. Many applied to the various orders of nuns and entered the convents. Most left within the first two years.

As the last six months in Brooklyn raced by, I had to apply to college and make decisions immediately, with little information. And, it turned out, my choices were limited because of the lack of modern language classes. "I refuse to go to a girl's school. I've had it with girls' schools," I emphatically told my parents when a couple of Catholic colleges were mentioned as their choices. Of course, I couldn't admit to not wanting a Catholic college to them. I really wanted to go to Radcliffe.

"You can't go to a Protestant school," Dad emphatically stated. Even though my Uncle Harry had offered to pay the Radcliffe tuition, Dad's pronouncement ended all discussion. It became more and more clear as the weeks sped by that my college choice would be my parents' decision.

I was seventeen when I left Brooklyn and my Catholic womb, full of excitement about a new world to explore. I don't know how Queens College became the choice. Certainly Dad let me know that he did not want me to leave his nest.

"You're too young to go away to school," Dad would pronounce.

"How come Jim can be away, and it'll be OK for Alice to be away next year?" I'd yell back. "You don't trust me, do you?"

I think the fact that Queens College was close to home and that I would once again be on a free ride – back then there was no tuition at the various city colleges – were the deciding factors. "Mary has always been a scholarship student," Dad always liked bragging.

I passed the admissions exam and was secretly thrilled that I had won the argument and wouldn't have to go to a Catholic school. But I was not thrilled that I wouldn't be living away from home. With my brother already at Glenclyffe High School in Garrison, New York, and one sister planning on boarding at nursing school the following year, that would leave my youngest sister just entering high school, and me, at home with Mother and Dad.

My high school nuns worried about the future of my soul. Rightfully so, it turned out! My parents had no idea about what Queens College was like at the time. All they knew was that the school had an outstanding academic reputation and there was no tuition. If they had any hint that it was a hotbed of liberal thought, that many of the faculty were suspected Communist sympathizers and that only ten percent of the student body was Christian, they would have probably made another choice.

I left the graduation ceremonies at Bishop McDonnell ready to fly, even though I was hobbled through the event with a bad case of sun poisoning. The weekend before graduation, my friends and I had continued our tradition of going to Jones Beach on Memorial Day, lathering ourselves with baby oil and baking on a blanket in the midday sun. At the end of a day, I was the only one sick with sun poisoning. I could hardly stand the touch of the graduation gown on my blistered legs as I shivered with feverish chills. I endured the long-winded ceremony, dying to get out of the overcrowded auditorium, away from the nuns and on with my life.

FAITH

Queens College

Little Red College Days

Stand on line, don't be shy.

Stand on line, try to look intelligent.

Stand on line; pretend you're used to this.

The first day of freshman registration at Queens College, I spent hours of standing, shifting from left to right foot, trying to shift my presentation from blasé to intense, to indifferent, to uncontrolled staring. I looked around the gym at what seemed like a stadium-size group of casually dressed students.

"Oh my gosh! That guy looks just like Jerry Lewis," I thought. In fact, there were a lot of guys who looked like that and a lot of girls with mounds of dark, thick, curly hair. Some of the blond familiar-looking girls were decked out in poodle skirts with matching neckerchiefs. There were a few cute crew-cut boys in chinos and white T-shirts, shuffling around in their cool loafers. But most of the guys had Brylcreemed hair and wore skinny pants and awful plaid shirts. In 1957 in Queens the only jeans we knew were worn in the movies, on Western ranches, and they were called "dungarees."

I had no idea how the registration system worked. A couple of friends from high school were with me as pals, but they were no help. Impatiently and with seventeen-year-old bravado, I moved along with the line, pretending I knew what I was doing. What I didn't know was that at the end of the line there would be a gruff guy telling me that calculus was overbooked and I had to take statistics instead.

"But I haven't had advanced algebra," I protested.

"Ignore it. You're in statistics. Next," he replied.

My first semester's credits would be all required courses. Along with the dreaded statistics, I signed up for English, French, general science, phys ed, music, art history, speech and a two-year course called Contemporary Civilization in the West. Next I followed the bookstore signs to one of the old Quonset huts on the campus. More lines to deal with, snaking around the little building, moving slowly, slowly into the store smelling deliciously of printing ink. I picked up pounds of textbooks, paid the bill and, more than five hours after the start of the day, headed to the cafeteria to meet one of my high school chums.

Built on what was originally a Dutch farm, the Queens College campus was at one time a home for delinquent boys, the New York Parental School. It was founded in 1907 by the Board of Education, according to the July 12, 1920, *New York Times*, to educate "boys between the ages of twelve and fifteen who steadily refuse to attend school … boys who seem so constructed that they cannot stay steadily in ordinary schools long enough to get the amount of education prescribed by their wise old Uncle Samuel to learn in this school, where sessions of schoolroom work are followed by stretches of farming or industrial training, and they are graduated, not from a parental or truant schools but from Public School No. –, and start in life without a handicap." Idyllic and idealistic, the school was closed in 1934 after the Queens district attorney brought brutality charges against the staff. The college opened in the fall of 1937.

The seventy-two-acre campus was a refuge for me. I was fascinated by the mix of old and new. Many of our classes were held in Spanish Mission architectural style buildings with stucco walls and red tiled roofs, leftovers from the Parental School. The newer buildings were sleek and functional. Even though it was in the middle of heavily populated Flushing in the hectic borough of Queens, it felt like a country estate, a place unto itself.

The day after registration, I met with my adviser in her small, dark den of an office, "Hello Miss Sheehan. Please sit down," Dr. Helen Gill Viljoen greeted me, all five feet of her rising courteously from her old wooden chair. She wore a purple smocked frock adorned with a large brooch, heavy stockings and sensible shoes. Her gray hair was swept up casually in a bun at the back of her neck. Little rolls of fat covered her from head to toe. I thought she was adorable. For the next four years, this eccentric, brilliant Victorian scholar was my touchstone, my cheering squad, my academic confessor.

She administered a writing test and told me, "My dear Mary, you have excellent grammar and punctuation. But you don't have one original thought on your paper. I don't want you to ever take a writing class, but we're going to have to teach you to express your own feelings and ideas."

The skills acquired at Bishop McDonnell through vigilant Catholic indoctrination about grammar had taken their toll on my right brain. In the next couple of years as I moved away from Catholic grammar – and rules – and with the always vigilant support of Dr. Viljoen, I decided to major in English and minor in philosophy. No, wait! English and art, or maybe English and music. I was tortured with wanting to do it all until the sophomore deadline day for declaring my major, finally choosing English as my major and philosophy as my minor course of study.

Those first two years were the most intense and exciting years of my young life as I struggled to find my voice and discovered my ability to question. Freshman year, the Contemporary Civilization in the West teacher presented a theme for a required term paper and unwittingly became my first guide on my journey from unconditional faith.

"One of your choices for a paper," Dr. Sakowitz said, "is a research paper on the historical life of Jesus."

"The historical life?" I thought. "I didn't know Jesus had a historical life ... he was just God."

I took on the topic. Dr. Sakowitz, amused by my naïveté, offered to help me through my research. I read, for the first time, Albert Schweitzer, Ernst Renan and David Strauss, comparing their theories on Jesus, the man. Fascinated by the readings, I threw myself into the research and wrote an A paper.

Meanwhile, I was on my way to failing statistics. Trying to understand this required math class was like trying to jump on a moving train. I had no idea, at all, of what I was trying to learn and, more importantly, no idea of how to ask for help. Pretending I knew what I was doing, I kept doing nothing until the end of the semester when I was faced with the first and last F in my young life.

Shame, fear, panic! How to tell my father the accountant that I had failed statistics! "Mother, Dad," I squeaked out one night after dinner. "I'm going to have to spend part of the summer in school because I failed statistics," I spit out as fast as I could. "But don't worry. I'll pay the tuition."

They were surprisingly calm, but agreed heartily that I was responsible for the tuition. There were a few of those comments from them about being "disappointed in you," but no yelling and screaming. Just guilt. Summer school was brief and painless and somehow I got a B the second time around, though I never did manage to understand the subject. However, I was beginning to understand how to play the game of grades.

After the first six months I became more used to the academic styles of my classmates. With the exception of science, classes were small, with at most thirty in each. No one stood to speak to the professor, a habit I had to quickly overcome after all those years of raising my hand, waiting to be called on and then standing respectfully to address "Sister." More shocking were the challenges I heard from my classmates questioning a professor's statement. I couldn't quite get the hang of what always seemed like the supremely confident and all-knowing response or retort.

Second-semester freshmen were allowed to join sororities and fraternities. Greek life was a big deal on this commuter campus, offering a base for students who spent a lot of time commuting to campus by subway, bus or, in a few cases, by car. Social life centered around these organizations, the cafeteria (the Caf), publications and clubs. Teams were in their infancy at the twenty-year-old campus. Athletics were not the first interest of most of the students, many of them first-generation children of the Holocaust, whose main goal was assimilation and professional success.

For a month or so during the Rush Period, we lowly freshmen were picked over like pigs in a pen by the various sororities or fraternities. We all knew which were the best ones, defined by power on the campus, size and appearance. We also knew which ones were Christian and which were for Jews, and that there was no crossing of lines between the two. There were two national sororities that I wanted to join, but Alpha Delta Pi was my favorite.

The Rush Tea for ADPi was a formal affair – snooty and pretentious, perfectly done by tea standards of the day. I shyly made my way around the rooms where the tea was held, interviewed one-on-one by attractive blonds with haughty accents. No Queens talk here. My mother would approve! I awkwardly tried to make smart small talk while balancing a teacup and a dainty sandwich in one hand. All the upperclassmen sisters seemed so polished, smart, beautiful and put together. Across the dining room, I spied one of the few non-blonds other than myself. Beautiful with dark brown curly hair, Nancy was a standout. We immediately knew we wanted to get to know each other.

That encounter amongst the soignée, slim blonds looking us over began a friendship of a lifetime. After a nerve-wracking week, to my delight and surprise, I received an invitation to pledge the two groups I coveted. Nancy and I compared notes and decided that we would both pledge ADPi, or AD Phew, as her father irreverently called it.

Sisters became our mentors, tutoring for classes, coaching on behavior and dress, teaching us pledges the national rules and regulations for an ADPi Girl. The Silver Tea, celebrating our formal initiation at the end of the semester, was a romantic and sentimental occasion, filled with flowers and candles and song, frilly dresses and tears. With great ceremony we pledged our commitment to scholarship, leadership, service to others and sisterhood. It was a throwback to 19th century southern life at Wesleyan Female College in Macon, Georgia, where ADPi was founded in 1851, the oldest secret society for women in the world's first women's college.

But the ADPi I joined didn't reside in a grand antebellum mansion on a tree-lined street. Our weekly meetings were held in an empty classroom, and our daily life outside classes centered in The Caf. Food was an accessory to the socializing and organizing that took place at grungy tables in uncomfortable chairs. I loved being with my sisters, but people who were different were becoming even more interesting.

I so wanted to meet some of my other new classmates. Every once in a while during an afternoon coffee break in The Caf between classes, I'd take a deep breath and wander over to one of their tables, with some phony excuse for getting to meet everyone. Before long I was often on the other side of The Caf where the more serious students hung out. Not only were they more serious, they were also not Christian and therefore enticing to me.

My new friends took me with them when Eleanor Roosevelt came to campus to talk about her recent trip to Moscow. At home, even the mention of her name started a torrent of hateful accusations, a rant about her challenging disagreements with Cardinal Spellman, the powerful and popular archbishop of New York. My father, the Teddy Roosevelt fan, had nothing good to say about "the other side of the family," ever since the Catholic Church decided that the former First Lady was a Communist sympathizer. I used the occasion as an opportunity to challenge my father, reporting to him that her speech was full of compassion and understanding of Soviet citizens as human beings. That set off an explosion, but I was beginning to enjoy those explosions. They gave me an opportunity to air the thinking of some of my newfound left-wing friends. More importantly, those sometimes verbally violent scenes at home were laying the groundwork for me to demonstrate my will.

When Allen Ginsberg came to the college for a poetry reading, I didn't know anything about him, but it was poetry, and I was an English major, so I knew I had to be there. I was delighted as I walked into the auditorium to see Ginsberg sitting on the edge of the stage, his legs dangling provocatively in front of his audience. He read, his companions read ... and read. And, to my amazement, he used the F word many times. I wasn't altogether sure I was ready for that, but I was ready for my new world.

By junior year I was swinging from one side of the campus to the other – from the "proper" sorority girls to the radical student-newspaper crowd. The newspaper became my home away from home when I joined the staff. It was there that I got to know an already eccentric, brilliant English major whom I had met in a Shakespeare class. We were drawn to each other, not sexually, but intellectually. We were known in the philosophy department as "Yin and Yang," apparently because we complemented each other in class discussion and writing.

Peter was a short, blond curly-headed Jewish boy from Queens who looked far younger and had lived far more years than his age. We loved reading poetry to each other. One night, to my great delight, he said, "Hey Sheehan, how about going to hear some poetry in the Village?" (He never addressed me by anything but my last name.) In the early '60s Greenwich Village coffee houses were inexpensive gathering places for poets and writers. I was convinced that some kind of writing would be my career. The drama and intensity I heard in those coffee houses– the sadness, torment, struggles, love stories – assured me this would be my life. Working on the newspaper and writing poetry, I was caught up in this romantic world of folks who were struggling to make ends meet while doing their art – and also, of course, drinking coffee and beer and cheap wine. They may have also been doing drugs, but I was unaware of that.

Putting on my best black skirt and sweater (since I thought all real creative writers only wore black), I'd meet Peter and, often joined by a few other intense types, walked the streets of the Manhattan center of Bohemian life searching coffee houses for the next great poet and playwright. Other nights I roamed those same streets with a fraternity guy, eating at some romantic little Italian café and enjoying Oscar Peterson, Charles Mingus, the Kingston Trio or Barbra Streisand in some dark nightspot.

I swung between the sacred and the profane those first two years, learning about me, learning about my talents, learning about sex and relationships. I dated everyone who asked me out at first, still so unaware, missing cues, trying too hard, but ever so curious. I was so well trained in humility, so uneducated and frightened about my sexuality that I was a pushover for any male who made a pass at me. Not knowing that sex was on the agenda for an evening, I would then often spend the end of the night fighting off an overheated college guy. Until I met a Holy Cross man who was a couple of years older than I. We were madly attracted to each other, even while I was dating other men.

As I began junior year, my parents sold our family home and moved to Coral Gables, Florida. My father was offered what seemed like an exciting adventure, opening new stores for the holding company he worked for. Ann went to Florida with Mother and Dad, but the rest of us were able to stay at our various academic institutions. At this time, Alice was attending nursing school and Jim was boarding in the minor seminary in Garrison. Finally, I was living independently from my parents, sharing an apartment funded by my father, with my cousins and my sister who came there some weekends. It was such a relief to be out of my parents' home. Even though they were paying my bills, I felt liberated and ready to explore my independence, no longer hampered by curfews and endless political arguments with my father.

Our apartment was the perfect setting for romance. One night with a full moon pouring in the windows of the oversized living room, "Tall, Dark and Handsome" convinced me to go "all the way," as the song goes. An accomplished tenor, my friend had been singing that Frank Sinatra song in my ear for months. Most of my Catholic no-no's about sex left me in the rush of romance and passion that night. It was a sweet and perfectly natural experience for me except that my obsessive self-criticism of my body was a big issue. After we made love, I quickly left the living room, shrouding my body in an oversized bath towel, ashamed to show my freckles, my flat chest, my big feet and every other real or imagined flaw. "Tall, Dark and Handsome," to his credit, always assured me I was flawless in his eyes.

I was more ready than ever for sexual exploration. I had been reading Simone de Beauvoir and was being coached by an upper classman, president of the student body, who had taken an unusual interest in me. Unbeknownst to me, he had the same unusual interest in a number of other Catholic girls. His mission was to convert all of us to atheism, sexual freedom and adventure, and to grow under his tutelage to become what he considered to be full open-minded women. I thought he was so interesting, so mature, so liberated, and so I willingly read the books, watched the films and attended the lectures he recommended.

He told me it would be a liberating growth experience for me to share his bed with him and another woman. I declined and then began to question his kinkiness and his motives. He was relentless, however, and pestered me for the next year, bringing me new books on the new thinking about womanhood, sex and relationships. I was scared. I was titillated. I was not sure of how to end this relationship. He graduated. That ended it … for a while … until he married and then came back into my life, urging me to explore a relationship with him and his wife. Again, I declined, this time with more conviction that he might be brilliant and certainly taught me a lot, but he was also crazy and not part of my plan.

Fully involved in the excitement of feminism, sexual freedom and civil rights, I was beginning to understand my own mind and will. I was an enthusiastic participant in anything that smacked of new thinking. Not only was I living away from my parents, but I was also so intellectually excited about my courses that I was overbooked with credits. I was president of the sorority at that point, involved on a faculty/student committee to visualize the future of the college as it became part of the City University of New York and writing for the newspaper, which was on a campaign against the Catholic bishop. I decided to run for office as the college's student council vice president, against a serious guy who was politically savvy and determined to win, on his way to becoming a lawyer. I was on complete overload. The campaign was hard and harsh. My Christian friends did not approve of my left-wing campaign and complained to me that I was "not running where I belonged." Translated, that meant I was not running on the conservative, mainly Catholic party, but rather on the liberal, mainly Jewish party. Their remarks were hurtful, but also empowering in a way. I was going to do what I was going to do. My will was at its most determined self.

After a grueling campaign, much more intense than I had bargained for, I lost the race for vice president. In the intensity of that campaign I forgot that I was also on the ballot to be elected as the college's representative to the National Student Association. To my surprise, I won that election. I'd be flying to Minneapolis as the delegate from Queens to the annual convention at the end of the summer. That was pretty exciting for me and a bonus that came unexpectedly after the vice presidential loss.

As junior year ended I was so weak and exhausted I could hardly get out of bed in the morning. I barely ate but continued smoking, of course, and got to as many classes as I could, taking as many finals as I could muster. I might have had a breakdown. But that was something that was never discussed in the family. My mother was informed that I was sick by the dean of women. They decided that I should spend the summer in Florida recuperating. I remember crying a lot during torrid, tropical days, sleeping a lot, drinking a lot of chocolate milkshakes rather than eating and not knowing what was wrong with me. The medical diagnosis was anemia. No one ever checked on my emotional or spiritual state. No one ever questioned if my immature self was ready for the heady life of the Little Red College. I seemed to be able to handle everything, but when everything became more than I could handle, I fell apart. I was scared, but knew I would get better. I was determined to return for senior year and finish with a bang.

In August I left my parents' home gratefully and flew from Miami to Minneapolis. The day before I left, Mother and I had one of a handful of sweet, gentle and intimate moments together. She took me shopping and, as we wandered through one of the stores Dad was working for, she said, "I'd like to buy you something special to take home with you for the year. Pick out anything you'd like." Amazed, I headed towards the lingerie department and made a beeline to a case of beautiful slips. I chose a Pucci design with ecru lace trim on the top and the hem, which I thought she might find too sexy. To my surprise, she said, "That's great, Mary. It's yours." Today, Mother's most intimate gift to me, that slip, sits in a drawer, wrapped in tissue.

Flying to Minneapolis, I was enthralled with the sight of the sun setting all the way there, convinced that its beauty was some kind of sign of promise for the year ahead. Arriving by taxi at the University of Minnesota, I was surprised by the heat and humidity of the evening and the massive number of students roaming about the campus. For the next week I was on a high, listening to impassioned speeches, voting on national student issues of the day, surrounded by new and different people. The only other Queens College person there was my opponent who had won the election. By this time I was fully recovered from my feeling of failure about the election and we enjoyed each other's company, played piano together in the evening, voted together and made plans for the upcoming year at the college.

The air in the meetings was vibrant with speeches and panels about civil rights and student rights, by members of the nascent Student Nonviolent Coordinating Committee. We sang or played or listened to music of the Kingston Trio, Peter Paul & Mary and Bob Dylan, all reflecting "The times they are a changin'."

I was assigned to share a dorm room with a blond girl from California for the week of the convention. I didn't quite understand what happened each night but finally got it after the third night when yet another guy came to our room to pick her up for dinner and she never returned until the next morning. I hated her and envied her and didn't quite understand her evening disappearing act. She was clearly having a great social time while I was having a great political time. She always missed the early morning speeches exhorting us to be leaders in the new world order.

Back in Queens I had a letdown after the excitement of the convention. I made a report to the student council, urging the college to become involved in the new civil rights movement and more aware of the issues of race and sex that were smacking up against us. My report was eagerly endorsed by the student council, and our Little Red College embraced the protest bandwagons as they came down the highway.

What should have been an easy senior year turned out to be very busy one. I had to catch up on the classes I missed at the end of junior year, prepping for exams in all the courses I had been taking the previous semester, as well as finishing up my senior courses for graduation. "Tall, Dark and Handsome "and I caught up with each other whenever he was home, and I continued my other social life in full swing. I was ready to leave the campus come May, although sad to leave my friends and the outstanding faculty. I planned to go on to graduate school and sought the advice of the dean who had been my medieval literature professor and was the graduate adviser for the English department.

My father demanded that I remain in New York for graduate school, although I really wanted to go to Wisconsin. Since he was paying for some of graduate school, and since I wasn't yet financially independent, I demurred again, and applied to New York University, which the dean had recommended to me. I never called upon my father's legacy at NYU but simply applied and was admitted to the English department.

I attended graduation ceremonies with Nancy and her family since neither of my parents was able to come. Nor did any of the rest of my family, which I now find curious. Where were they all? Were they invited? Were they just busy? What did they think of me and my achievement? Even though I was far from the first to graduate college, I had done it, after all!

No summer vacation for me except for a trip to Cape Cod for a long weekend with a bunch of graduating ADPi sisters. We had a raucous time roaming beaches and bars, full of graduation joy and excited about our futures. A few days later my reality was clear. I had to start pounding the pavement. It was time to find a job "in magazines." I had a summer job again, thanks to Dad, but I expected I would be leaving it shortly to start my real career.

FAITH

The Single Girl Life

ON BEING "IN MAGAZINES"

As my English major pals were heading for graduate school, teaching jobs or marriage and home, all seemingly on a clear path, I was struggling with publishing company exams. My dream of "working in magazines" was shaky.

In that merry month of May 1961, unemployment hit 7.1 percent. The country was at the tail end of a brief recession. I didn't know anything about economic cycles, but I did realize that finding a job was not going to be easy.

My parents and just about everyone else assumed I would be a teacher. After all, Mother taught high school English. Grandma had once been a teacher. The acceptable career paths for Catholic girls – actually, for most girls in that time – were teaching and nursing and marriage. Having chosen literature over music as my college major, I decided that teaching would be dreary compared to the romantic and exciting life "in magazines." I set my sights on getting hired at *Time* magazine or *The New Yorker*.

When the job market turned out to be brutal, I signed up with an employment agency. Sitting beside a gray metal desk in a dingy office suite near Times Square, I nervously signed a piece of paper agreeing to pay the agency a fee for finding me my perfect first job.

All that summer in the pounding heat of New York City without air-conditioning, I was sent out to publishing houses, including giants like McGraw-Hill and Time-Life. I waited for my interview in their surprisingly unimpressive reception rooms with uncomfortable bland brown and gray upholstered chairs and sofas. Increasingly, "Miss Sheehan, please follow me" triggered a moment of insecurity as I was led into a testing room by a serious staffer. The tests themselves focused on grammar and proofreading abilities. It felt like a lot of scrutinizing for entry-level work as an editorial assistant. I didn't tell anyone how disappointed I was that I wasn't interviewing with the likes of William Shawn or any of the other leading editors of the time.

I usually talked to someone in personnel who had the air of one who was bored and bombarded with job applications. I steadfastly declined assistance from my family or friends of the family, having no idea about networking. It was more important to find a job on my own, I thought, fearing that someone would embarrass me by doing a favor I really didn't deserve. I was determined to be in charge of my own destiny. Four months and many dead ends later, after all my college friends were comfortably ensconced in their classrooms, I got a job. It paid $65 a week.

I arrived wearing my modest gray interview suit at the splendid offices of the Institute of Radio Engineers, located at 1 East 79th Street, on the corner of Fifth Avenue in what was once the Brokaw Mansion, to meet The Editor. I thought I was hot stuff as I mounted the marble staircase, trying my very best to walk and breathe as if I were accustomed to the sumptuous surroundings. The flamboyant 19th century mansion was inspired by the 16th century French Chateau de Chenoncess. Designed for the clothier Isaac Brokaw by Rose & Stone, it faced Central Park and was flanked up Fifth Avenue and down 79th Street by two equally impressive mansions that he built for his children. It was in the rarified neighborhood of the Stuyvesant Mansion, built by a descendant of Peter Stuyvesant, and the Duke Mansion, built for James Buchanan Duke, a founder of the American

Tobacco Company, and the home for many years of his daughter, the socialite Doris Duke.

The mansion and its accompanying buildings had been purchased by the Institute of Radio Engineers in the 1930s. The grand staircase led to institute's third -floor publications offices where the Editor-from-Hell greeted me from behind her cluttered desk in front of windows looking out onto the park. Helene Frischauer wasn't exactly frumpy and she wasn't exactly glamorous and she wasn't exactly friendly. Tall and slim and dark, she was tight-faced and very, very serious. Only the huge fireplace in the room was welcoming. I was terrified.

The Institute of Radio Engineers (IRE) was founded in 1912 as an international society for scientists and engineers involved in the development of wireless communications. Marconi and Edison were its original gods. Radio was the first miracle. The IRE was set up so that scientists around the world could keep up with the 20th century's vast technological changes. The society's dozen or more publications were the primary vehicle of communication among its professionals. Papers were published, and letters and responses to papers flowed around the world of engineers through the *Proceedings* and *Transactions* of the IRE. In the 1960s the society caught up with the times and changed the name of the organization to the IEEE, the Institute for Electrical and Electronic Engineers.

In this magnificent office I was entering, all its *Proceedings* and *Transactions* were written and edited, then designed and prepared for publication. There was an impressive body of work about biochemical engineering, mechanical engineering, all kinds of engineering. It was a world I knew nothing about. I had merely satisfied their college requirement for one year of science. The handsome and highly illustrated magazines were produced monthly and quarterly by a staff of thirteen editorial assistants, two editors and a secretary. I was offered a position as one of those thirteen editorial assistants.

I was "in magazines!"

It was at the IRE that I learned how to edit. The thirteen of us were all young women. We sat in a big and no longer beautiful room, each at a gray metal desk with an electric typewriter and telephone. It was sort of like a newsroom of its day, although calmer and more orderly. Most of the time. We had a slightly distant park view from the front windows, perfect for gazing out and daydreaming, less conducive to deadlines. Editor Frischauer's glass-enclosed office was at the front of the floor, never far from our desks. A mysterious and rarely seen managing editor, the only man in the building, had an office on the other side of the staircase. We worked 9 to 5 with an hour for lunch.

My best friends were Lila, a homely, sweet and intensely bright Jewish girl, an English major from Hunter College, and Priscilla, a tall, rigid and conservatively dressed WASP, a religion major from Wheaton College. We loved doing the *New York Times* crossword puzzle. We hid the puzzles on our laps and furtively filled them in during the day. For lunch, we darted across Fifth Avenue with our brown bags to the Metropolitan Museum of Art and quickly ate the sandwiches we brought before exploring a new exhibit or an old favorite like the Greek and Roman hall at that grand and free institution. It was always a glorious break.

Editor Frischauer assigned us manuscripts from contributing engineers. We had no say in her choices. Novice assistants were given the less complicated manuscripts to edit and galleys to proofread. Only experienced assistants received the longer, more difficult works with illustrations that also needed preparation. And only occasionally were the very experienced assistants allowed to talk to a real author. That task was usually the distinct honor of Editor Frischauer, who never failed to impress upon us the importance of the authors and the lowliness of our positions. It was only after I'd been there a year that I was given the honor of talking to an author who, as luck would have it, was a growly old guy from Minnesota.

Not only did I learn editing skills from the Editor-from-Hell, I also was introduced to the basics of layout and design. In six months I was promoted to handle the news section of the monthly publication. I worked on stories from information she gave me, finding the appropriate art. When the content was ready for layout, I arranged the stories and art on large dummy pages. This often meant moving around snippets of copy on long galley sheets, endlessly trying to figure out how to get each page set up. Often during this tortuous process, The Editor would swing past my desk on her rounds and check out my work. If she didn't like it, she swept all the copy that was gingerly tacked onto the dummy page in minuscule pieces to the floor and say, "Do it again," in her stentorian voice. On my hands and knees with my face burning with embarrassment, I crawled around to collect all the galley pieces and start over again. The demeaning and strict atmosphere of the office, rather than the work, spurred me to start job hunting again.

My parents, who had returned to Queens after my father's adventure in Florida fizzled, insisted that I live with them again. I gave up the apartment I shared with my cousins and returned home unwillingly but with no choice since I wasn't making enough money to live on my own. The pressure to obey them was more than I could resist right then, but I was determined to make living at home again a short-term arrangement.

"I've paid off the employment agency," I told my friends, "and it's time to go on to something that pays me enough so I can move out of home and will be a little more exciting than engineering news and manuscripts."

It was Gloria Golden, a friend and Alpha Delta Pi sorority sister, who led me to *Harper's Bazaar* in 1963. A talented art major a couple of years ahead of me at school, Golden, as she was known, had landed a job in the production department at the magazine right out of college. By the time I graduated, she had already been named production editor of *Bazaar*.

I was whining about my IRE job at a party of sorority sisters when Golden told me of an opening at *Harper's Bazaar*. She set up an interview with one of the editors who was looking for an assistant. I had never read the magazine, so I immediately bought a copy. I spent the next week trying to figure out how to translate engineering to fashion and talking with Golden for hours, getting up to speed on this new world.

The Skinny On
The Fashion Magazine

That successful interview with the promotion director is a blur. I was so thrilled at being in this famous New York building on 56th Street and Madison Avenue that the details escape me. The fact that the offices were grungy and crowded and noisy only added to the glamour in my eyes. "F. Scott Fitzgerald must have worked in offices like this," I dreamily imagined as I entered the slow old-fashioned elevator to the eleventh floor for my interview.

I was hired on the spot, at $75 per week, $10 more than I'd been earning, and was asked to report to *Harper's Bazaar* in two weeks. Oh happy day! I could now stand up against any of my college classmates who had been toiling for two years in real jobs with real salaries and proudly announce where I was working. Of course, I wouldn't tell them I was making a pittance compared to their teaching salaries. No more trying to explain why editing engineering manuscripts was significant work. Everyone knew about the importance of *Bazaar*, didn't they?

The first day on the job I was paraded around the editorial and advertising offices by the promotion department. I felt frumpy and fat. Did they know I was from Queens and that I had no money, I wondered? Did they know I was a babe in the woods in their work? Did they know I had hardly read the magazine? And what did "promotion and merchandising" mean, anyway? Actually, most of the top editors were so self-involved, they hardly glanced at me, this new kid in promotion and merchandising. At that time, that department didn't have the clout that editorial had, nor did it offer the huge paychecks that advertising did. That would change as the editorial pages came to rely on the promotion and merchandising of their contents. The publisher was a whiz at sales and developed a track record of constantly increasing advertising and promotion revenues to support the editorial content. While the editorial staff sometimes railed against his commitments and deals with advertisers, they were enjoying the fruits of his labors as increased revenues gave them more resources for choice talent and travel to exotic places that they once couldn't afford.

My new professional arena housed two merchandising editors, two editorial assistants, the promotion director and her assistant, and an art and production department. About twenty people in all, we reported both to the publisher and the editor but came under the publisher's budget. As an editorial assistant, I got to go along on junkets in the garment center, meet the folks who made the gorgeous clothing and accessories we displayed in the magazine and write promotion copy. I also got to work twelve-hour days, haul the gorgeous clothing and accessories back and forth for photo shoots, pick up the sweaty gorgeous clothing that was strewn around the studio during and after the photo shoot, sort and find all the missing accessories, get coffee for the editor and the photographer and the model and anyone else who was around at any given moment, order and pick up lunch and cigarettes, schedule everything for my editor and answer the office phone. I was in my professional heaven. I was bowled over by the beauty, fashion, fame, talent, wealth, snobbery and bitchiness I encountered every day.

I was still living with Mother and Dad, unable to afford my own place. In the early 1960s, single women either stayed at home until they married or doubled, tripled or quadrupled up in an apartment not unlike a college dorm. I wanted none of that. I needed to be on my own, to learn about myself, to take risks, on my own. My chance to do that came in the person of Sandra McPeak, the daughter of the British publisher of *Bazaar UK*, who was in New York on a yearlong internship and about to return to London. We met in the publisher's office and liked each other instantly. When she told me she had an apartment ten blocks from the office on Madison Avenue and had to give up her lease, we devised an elaborate plan. I lied to my parents, telling them I'd found a roommate in Manhattan and was taking my own place. My parents were not happy with this arrangement. After I had successfully escaped their nest, I told them my roommate had to return to London. Part of that story was true – I just didn't tell them I knew she would be leaving the country shortly before I even moved into her apartment, and I would be living alone.

Mother and Dad had a strong reaction: no conversation, no support and no encouragement. For the next six months I was in deep trouble with them. Mother and I had perfunctory telephone conversations. Dad refused to speak to me. My two dear aunts, Mother's two sisters who babysat for us when we were young, came to my aid, supplying me with much affection along with domestic necessities. Aunt Ceal arrived one night for dinner, giddy with delight that she was disobeying my mother, her older sister.

"I brought you some placemats I made for you," she said, "in case you want to have your friends in for dinner. There's some extra flatware in this bag that I had lying around my place. And, oh, here are some hand towels I embroidered years ago." Her sister, my Aunt Peg, came over on a Saturday, angered by my mother's lack of support, bringing more dishes, a couple of trays, gourmet food for the pantry, a bottle of Scotch and one of her own oil paintings that I last saw hanging in my grandparents' home.

My aunts were both in their fifties, living alone in separate apartments in Brooklyn after their parents died. They had enjoyed and endured their Post World War II careers and social lives and were loyal to the family, always interested in the lives of their many nieces and nephews. Not only had they been my babysitters, they had taken me to the opera for the first time, introduced me to new foods and new restaurants, shopped with me, talked about their professional work with enthusiasm and charm, invited me for overnights at their apartments and subsidized travel, beginning with my first trip to Ireland.

They never stopped supporting me. Peg would remain single throughout her life, ever faithful, the story goes, to the memory of a man she loved who died in the war. Ceal had just married a widower, her first marriage, and was having the happiest days of her life.

I needed their support as I learned unforgettable life lessons in the years I lived in my apartment. How to pay the rent every month without bouncing the check to the haughty and mean landlord Mr. Selwyn; how to eat dinner when the pantry was bare, truly bare; how to share whatever I had with my friends who were struggling to grow up as well; how to take joy in the little things like watching the pigeons on my "patio," which was an extension of the roof below; how to be street smart walking to work and feeling safe when I came home late at night and closed the firm brass door behind me. My neighborhood was rich in New York history, rich in famous and infamous residents, alive all the time except Sunday morning when no one seemed to move in the streets. At one time my grandmother and Dad had lived there.

That was the selling point that gave my father the excuse he needed to stop being mad at me. Besides that, he missed me. After about six months, my parents finally responded to my many dinner invitations. As Dad walked into the living room he noted, "This place is a fire trap." I knew he loved it. "I was a delivery boy for that pharmacy on the corner," he said after he had examined the place and enjoyed my dinner as fond memories of his youth in the same neighborhood returned.

The pages of *Harper's Bazaar* in those days of the '60s reflected the world we were enjoying, a world of hair teased and colored and blow-dried beyond human hair possibilities, astronauts and the beginnings of space exploration, thigh-high boots, very, very short dresses, new fibers replacing cotton and wool and silk, new music, new hope and new excitement. It was the fashion time of Richard Avedon, Twiggy, Jeanne Shrimpton, Diana Vreeland, Rudi Gernrich, Hiro, Andre Courreges, Mainbocher, Melvin Sokolsky, Pauline Trigere, John Fairchild, Francesco Scavullo, Nancy White. I wore beautiful knockoffs of Chanel and other French and American designers, which, even though they were knockoffs, still would cost a fortune if purchased at Saks Fifth Avenue. Another impoverished staffer introduced me to Ann Stalling, a transplanted Southern Black woman, who, from her Queens home, produced perfect copies from the fashion samples. I wore suits with severe lines in luxurious fabrics, dresses in geometric shapes, high heels and boots with pointy toes, garishly ornamented stockings, sumptuous evening wear, always sexy lingerie and always gloves, especially on the subway as Mother and my aunts had told me. (Gloves were the '60s version of hand sanitizer.)

Clothing was generously distributed to editors who pleased the designer or owner of a company. My jewelry came on loan from the accessories office that was always loaded with costume jewelry kept on hand for photo shoots. We had to look the part of the fashion expert, but some of us had to do it on the cheap, borrowing things and having copies made.

There was an abundance of talent at the very top levels in the creaky old Hearst Magazines building. I was in pretty amazing company and am forever touched by the brilliance that surrounded me then. We worked in dirty, small offices reeking of cigarettes, each of which bore the fashion mark of its occupant editor and editorial assistant. The only spacious offices were the domains of the publisher and of the editor. Four of us were lined up in our room – two of us, editorial assistants, in the front of the room protecting our two editors from unwanted intruders. There was no air conditioning in the building except for the open windows. Many a hot summer day in the city I remember sweating uncomfortably at my desk, forearms sticking to the soot-covered work on the desk in front of me. Thankfully, Henry Helper's drugstore on the ground floor kept us in sodas and iced coffee.

Our editors were highly recognizable. They were the women who wore their hats all day long. At our weekly editorial meetings, Nancy White, the editor in chief, would preside from behind her white French provincial desk, dressed to the nines, often in Chanel suit, a chic cigarette holder between her third finger and the stump of her index finger. I never knew what happened to that index finger, but I could hardly keep my eyes off the swaying cigarette holder during those meetings. Thirty of us gathered in her office, sitting on the floor or perched on gilt chairs, smoking and discussing the editorial and promotional content and themes of the upcoming issue. Discussing isn't really the right word. Voices were raised as egos clashed over the pages being created. There was always high drama.

And there was always a crisis – with a photographer, an art director, a manufacturer – or the copy was late, the garment was not delivered in time for a photo shoot, the model was out of control or fighting with the photographer, the editor was in a snit. During it all, Miss White, as she was always referred to, would calmly preside, firmly giving direction and soothing delicate egos so that the work would be complete and on time. I don't ever remember a month when the deadline was not an issue, and yet the magazine hit the newsstands on time every time.

I made a friend of a lifetime during those days. We don't remember how we met, but we do regale each other with memories of that magazine world. We worked on a few projects together and took breaks from the intensity, meeting in the dreary stairwell to groan or giggle about some crisis or annoyance around us. My dear friend lived one street uptown from me, just off Madison Avenue. We came from strikingly different families. She was raised on the Upper East Side of Manhattan, the granddaughter of a successful national retailer. My grandfather owned a small town general store. She was from great wealth. I was from the middle class. We both had intelligent, well-educated parents and domineering professional fathers. We were both English majors. We were the same age. She was short and dark. I was tall and fair. We just loved each other. We spent many evenings together, sharing small meals, cigarettes and Scotch and our secret sex-in-the-city life of the '60s, admittedly a much milder version of the current one. On Saturdays we headed over to our Lexington Avenue grocery store, returning our deposit bottles. She, the daughter of wealth, would lead me through the aisles, pointing out the bargains, allowing no frivolous spending.

Our friendship grew during those years, nurtured by our life interests and our values, by our work and our social lives. We were desperate together and joyful together, as women in their twenties can be. She was one of the first friends to whom I would confess my most significant tale of love. We spent many a night of weeping and railing at her apartment or mine as I struggled through my most complex relationship.

I was promoted at *Bazaar* from mere editorial assistant to assistant to the promotion director Berta MacDonald. She was an elegant divorced older woman who wouldn't meet anyone's vision of a fashion magazine principal except for her expensive clothing and jewelry. She was probably in her sixties, short and chubby, with a gruff manner. The only memorable moments I recall of her are long and loud battles with the publisher and all the editorial staff. She had a winter getaway in Scottsdale as well as her beautiful apartment on Sutton Place.

One afternoon shortly after I started working for her, I was suddenly asked to report to the publisher's office. I went to his suite, notebook in hand. I had only met him when he came to my boss's office for one of their late afternoon feuds. William M. Fine introduced himself and always seemed very interested in what I was doing. I noticed that he was rather good looking, but he was so important in my eyes that I could only mutter a few shy responses to his questions. I went to his suite, notebook in hand. I was told by his ever-faithful assistant Alice to go to into Mr. Fine's office, which I did, notebook and pen primed for instructions.

"Miss Sheehan," he said after a few introductory pleasantries, "I want you to meet me for dinner tonight at 7 o'clock at Romeo Salta, and we can discuss your future at the magazine."

"Yes, sir, of course," I replied, not knowing how else to respond nor what I was responding to. I was so shocked I didn't mention it to anyone except my former officemate, a sweet, not-too-bright young socialite. "What should I do?" I asked Judy. She thought our publisher's request was odd as well but agreed that I had to go along with the assignment or I might be in trouble.

I took my notebook to the dinner rendezvous. Bill Fine was there ahead of me, nursing a drink at one of the banquettes towards the back of the restaurant. He acknowledged the notebook, which I thought meant he was impressed by my professionalism. I later found that he was rather charmed by my naïveté. I didn't understand why this giant figure wanted to know what my career plans were, what I thought about him, what I thought about other people at the magazine, what I thought about him, about him, about him. He explained to me that he was watching my work, wanted to guide my career, and that I should try out various departments to see which I most liked, let him know where I wanted to work and he would make it happen for me. In the meantime, he wanted me to move in to his office complex as a kind of special assistant until the new promotion director was hired. I didn't know my current boss had been fired until that moment. I was to begin immediately, reporting to his office the next morning to write and learn more about the magazine and the corporation. I would go to meetings with him in the garment center and to corporate offices as he pitched potential advertisers. I would also, upon his request, edit his son's school papers and continue meeting him for dinner. It was all too much for me to comprehend. My heart was racing. My brain was racing. I had no idea how to demur. I chastised myself for having any suspicious thoughts about his intentions.

We met on a regular basis for dinner, where he dumped all his problems on me. At one dinner he actually said the words, "My wife doesn't understand me." I almost choked on my asparagus, laughing at the trite line. He said he was offended by my response. I was beginning to get it.

A few months later we were walking up Fifth Avenue after dinner and came upon a landmark Doubleday bookstore. "Let's go in," he said. "I want to buy you a gift." He picked out a newly published book on the letters of F. Scott Fitzgerald, knowing I was fond of Fitzgerald, inscribing it, "To Mary, who thinks deeply and reacts with truth. WMF." We left the store and continued walking uptown. I thought maybe he was planning to walk me home. Usually, he put me in a cab after dinner. Instead, this night he began a quasi-internal dialogue, saying out loud, "I know I shouldn't ask you because you're an employee. But I'd love you to come to my apartment for an after-dinner drink so we can continue talking. You know I love talking with you. We have such interesting conversations." I said nothing. He didn't notice since he was so involved in his conversation with himself. When he forcibly took my elbow and steered me towards Park Avenue, I knew we were heading across 59th Street toward his apartment at the Hotel Delmonico on Park Avenue and 59th Street.

"Just keep going," I said to myself. "Let's see where this leads." I was surprisingly unafraid, trusting myself and bemused by this man's confusion. When we arrived at his place, the doorman greeted him and ignored me. "Wonder if he's used to this," I thought. He poured us a couple of best label Scotch and waters, and we continued talking about literature. Suddenly he stood up, walked towards me, took my hand gently, pulled my up from my chair to embrace me, saying, "I know I shouldn't be doing this…"

From deep inside me a very responsible adult arose and said, "No, you shouldn't be doing this, and I should be leaving." It was probably an old movie script that I remembered. I headed for the door and said good night. He didn't resist.

The next day, everything in the office seemed the same. But it wasn't, of course. We continued to have dinner regularly. He continued his lustful inner musings about me and was eminently professional with me during days at the magazine. That is, until the week I left the magazine, when he behaved like a jilted jealous lover by demanding super human work and inflicting authority when I needed support.

Faith

About Priesthood

NUMQUAM SOLUS CUM SOLA, CUM SOLO

Never One Male with One Female or One Male

While the institution wasn't luxurious, Father Scanlan told me, it was well appointed and comfortably situated on 200 acres on the North Shore of Long Island. A Byzantine tower dominated the Spanish Romanesque main building of the Immaculate Conception Seminary, at the edge of an exclusive community in Lloyd Harbor. From the campus above Cold Spring Harbor and Oyster Bay, the Empire State Building in Manhattan was clearly visible thirty miles away.

In 1930, reverence for the priesthood was so strong that the entire $2.5 million project was fully paid for when it opened by the parishioners of the sprawling, ever-growing Diocese of Brooklyn. The first class of twenty-three seminarians was ordained to the priesthood in 1934. In 1946 there were one thousand forty-one Roman Catholic diocesan priests in the archdiocese. By 1953, the year before Father William Scanlan was ordained, more than five hundred – the rising generation of the Brooklyn diocesan clergy – had received all or part of their seminary training at Lloyd Harbor.

The diocese established in 1853 included parishes in the whole of Long Island, which served about fifteen thousand Catholics then. That number multiplied into the millions as the immigrant population of New York swelled throughout the first century of the diocese. Students were educated to become priests in this specific geographic area, a diocese, where they would perform various forms of ministry in that diocese, primarily as parish priests. A priest could also serve as a teacher, a diocesan administrator or chaplain in a hospital, prison or college.

The priesthood was a noble profession then. The quintessential successful Catholic family portrait included a son a priest, a son a doctor, a son a lawyer, a daughter a nun and all the rest of her sisters happily married. The mother of a priest was revered.

It was the Trappist monks who inspired young William. Their life of prayer and work and simplicity, in pursuit of the perfect life, in pursuit of virtue and a life lived for the glory of God, was an ideal that he aspired to when, in high school, he came upon the writings of Father Mary Raymond, a monk in the Trappist Abby of Gethsemane. William was so attracted to those spiritual ideals and particularly the book "The Man Who Got Even With God" that he began a correspondence with the charismatic Father Raymond. Their letters, now long disappeared, reflected William's intense desire to leave his Catholic high school and enter the monastery in Gethsemane under the guidance of Father Raymond. He applied and was accepted, pending his pastor's letter of recommendation.

The day came when his pastor called him and his father to the rectory to discuss that letter. To his astonishment, the pastor berated William, accusing him of trying to dodge the draft by applying to the monastery, scolding him about the foolishness of his desire, insisting instead that the boy attend the diocesan preparatory seminary. Unbeknownst to him, the pastor had slipped William's father a letter of recommendation, telling him not to let the young man know that he had written it and instructing him to watch and see how his son adjusted to the diocesan school. If William still wanted to be with the Trappists after a year, his father could surprise him with the pastor's referral. That moment never happened, William never asked about it again. Years later, his father confessed that he had conspired with the pastor.

Disappointed but determined in his pursuit of excellence, William enrolled in the preparatory seminary, graduated and moved on to seminary. He was ferociously committed to becoming a virtuous priest. He studied hard, and he loved the life of the seminary. He was on a path with clear markers, and he was an easy rider on that path. There was such assurance in the rule and in the promise of grace. For him and many of his classmates, the early 1950s were a time of intellectual and spiritual stimulation. The curriculum was a lofty means to an idealistic end. "We had a rule and a ritual for everything in the day," William said. "It was very comforting."

The rector of the seminary, the Reverend Patrick J. Barry, was a lordly man, a graduate of Trinity College in Dublin, trained for the priesthood at the renowned Maynooth Seminary. He fancied himself a Renaissance man, eager to bring cultural enlightenment to his students. On Sunday nights, guests performed music and gave talks on art and literature. "It was where I first enjoyed Mozart," Father Scanlan recalled to me one evening, "I never heard music like this at home."

He also fondly remembered the traditional Gaudeamus (from the Latin *gaudeo*, meaning "let us rejoice"). Because he was an Irishman, the Rector permitted this event only on St. Patrick's Day, to honor the mythological saint, and on the day before the seminarians went home on Christmas break. The Head Man, a seminarian appointed by the Rector to be the leader of the students, would ask permission for the event, and the students would create a musical comedy, a satirical commentary on life in the seminary. The tone was often venomous, perhaps because it was one of the very few opportunities for seminarians to express their displeasure or criticism of the system. It was a day of fun and rejoicing, a party for people who didn't really know how to party. Nor were they encouraged to. Their seminary life was about discipline and sacrifice.

There was never any discussion of sexuality. However, *"numquam solus cum sola"* – "never one male with one female" – was drummed into William's consciousness in those seminary days. This cardinal rule was stressed emphatically and continuously, an irrefutable standard for priestly life. William never questioned or challenged it.

In the early years after his ordination, Father was in his parish office when an attractive parishioner, an airline stewardess, came to the door asking him to bless a medal she was wearing. He carefully stood in the doorway of the room, preventing her from entering, blessed the medal and turned to re-enter his office. Flirtatiously, she asked him, "Father, would you put it around my neck?" "No dear, I don't think I'd better do that," he replied with a blush. He handed the medal back to the woman and returned to his office, closing his door. He had successfully sidestepped two moments of temptation – being alone with a woman in a room and touching a woman's body.

Numquam solus cum sola was a guide for a priest's life. And, in fact that standard governed Father's life from his ordination in 1954, until we met in 1966.

There was the other rule: *"Numquam solus cum solo"* – never one male with one male. A student was never to be alone with another seminarian, never to be in a circumstance that might lead to what was known as "a particular friendship." Each priestly candidate had his own bedroom and bath so that there would be no temptation for inappropriate personal contact. He was forbidden to visit in another student's room without direct permission from the faculty prefect residing on each floor.

On daily walks around the grounds of the large manor home where the seminarians lived for anywhere from four to six years, the young men were instructed to begin walks alone, taking up with whomever they met on the path as a companion for that walk. Wanting to cultivate friendships, however, and in violation of that rule, William and his classmates would make arrangements prior to walking time so that it would appear that they had accidentally bumped into each other. "Charlie, meet me at the bench over near that oak tree at 2:45," he would whisper to a friend after class. A few hours later, he and Charlie, or John or Sully, would meet "by chance" and walk together for the remainder of their free time.

There may not have been any discussion about sexuality, but celibacy was the elephant in the room from the moment a young man decided to become a priest. The promise of celibacy was the culmination of total willingness to serve the church. As Father painstakingly explained to me one evening shortly after we met, diocesan priests make no vows, unlike priests of religious congregations such as the Franciscans or Jesuits. A diocesan priest freely makes promises of celibacy and obedience to his bishop at ordination, but without vows.

At the end of the first year of theology (the year after college), William and his class were ordained subdeacons of the church. Informally known as "the Ritual of the Iron Pants," the ceremony began as thirty twenty-four-year-old men processed into the chapel, incense wafting through the sanctuary, each wearing an alb and a cincture and carrying the maniple and the dalmatic symbols of their new rank. They lay prostrate on the altar in front of the bishop. At a signal, they rose and, one by one, approached the bishop sitting on a footstool at the top of the altar. Holding the bishop's hand, the candidate was given the instruments of the office of subdeacon and committed to celibacy and obedience and to reading the divine office each day. This was the culmination of the seminarian's total willingness to serve the church. And this was the moment that, facing "the Ritual of the Iron Pants," some of them left the seminary.

In 1948, when William entered the seminary at the age of twenty, I was in the third grade at St. Teresa Little Flower Elementary School. The man I met in 1966, eighteen years later, exuded self-confidence.

The woman he met was still in the early stages of developing self-confidence. The synergy between us was immediate and strong. Perhaps I felt safe with this man because of his priesthood. He was an untouchable for a girl from my clan. And perhaps he felt safe with me as well, secure in his conviction and lifelong practice of abstinence and celibacy. But, no longer "*numquam cum sola.*"

REMEMBERING MEN
OF THE CLOTH

Charlie's death made me think of all of them, the men of the cloth whom Father had grown up with in seminary, with whom he shared vacations, played sports and enjoyed theater – the good times that pals spend together. "Once a priest, always a priest" was the rule, as was "once a Catholic, always a Catholic." Even those men who shed the cloth were forever considered brother priests.

Many years after his seminary days, Father told me that he could never understand why he and his fellow priests became immediate successes and important persons at the age of twenty-six, without having done anything except study. I never knew any of Father's pals to be other than gentle men, a pretty normal bunch of guys who chose a career that they considered a calling. The only career promise out of the ordinary that was made at ordination was to a celibate manhood.

Hugh

The confessor for Father's cataclysmic admission that he needed to leave the priesthood was the beloved Benedictine monk whom he talked with on his annual retreat. The monk's incredible and unexpected response to Father's confessions was, "I don't know how you guys do it. You lead such lonely lives." Hugh was referring to the contrast between the monastic life he lived where community was a way of life and the non-communal isolated life of a diocesan priest. Overwhelmed by the offer of forgiveness, and with the joy of being accepted, Father asked me to have lunch with Hugh. "You will love him, Mary," Father said. "He's a poet and a philosopher."

We met for lunch at a restaurant overlooking the Hudson River. I loved him immediately. The lanky, bald, beautiful middle-aged black-robed monk wanted to know who I was. He was concerned about my comparative youth. He challenged me to determine if I was prepared for the difficult days ahead for Will and me. Hugh gave me courage then and gave us courage and love for years to come.

A few years later he came to our farmhouse to work on his Ph.D. dissertation – a collection of his poetry – and to try to come to terms with his own priesthood. He read his poems to me while I took care of our newborn. He tended our vegetable garden and made luscious meals from newly discovered vegetarian cookbooks. When Will came home in the evening, he and Hugh talked and laughed and sang for hours.

Hugh had fallen in love with a divorced woman and didn't know what he wanted to do. Even the monastic life wasn't a barrier to this woman. He had been her confessor, and he became overwhelmed. After a few months he left us, joining her in California. We put Hugh in touch with friends and family in California and then we lost touch. He did finish his thesis, sent me a copy of it – his beautiful poems – and then he disappeared. He never married, returning to the Benedictines, living out his life in that community.

Charlie

I met Charlie before I met Father. Charlie was the chaplain of the Newman Center at Queens College, reputed to be a wild liberal. A big man with a belly laugh, he was very bright and very open with the students who joined the Newman Center. I was not one of them in my student days, being deliberately sectarian. However, I attended some of his very courant liturgies and was impressed with his modernism. He was a man of elegant tastes in food and wine and music and art. He loved conversation, the more controversial the better. He inspired young Newman Center members with his openness to new ideas, his fierce ability to defend an argument. He probably would never have survived the leftist culture of the college had he not been hip. Even the more traditional Catholic students were almost-liberals.

Lovable and aloof at the same time, he could never go quite as far left as Father did in his thinking but was fascinated by Father's intellectual courage. His affinity for drink seemed to take over his life as the loneliness of priesthood crept into his days. There was a woman, but he never laid aside the garb of priesthood. After he died in a nursing home in Florida when he was in his seventies, Father organized the memorial service at the seminary where they had all grown up.

Jimmy

Dear, sweet, intense Jimmy was the only man of the cloth who joyfully came to our wedding, dressed proudly in his "clerics," as the black suit, rabat and Roman collar were called. I had only seen him in jeans before that day – his statement to his bishop and his fellow priests about his lifestyle. A friend of the Berrigans and other radical clergy of the day, he ran a community center in Brownsville, then a most corrupt, poor and dangerous section of Brooklyn. I met him when a friend needed help.

My friend Michael King was writing a story on Brownsville for the *New York Times Magazine*. In order to escape his inept seduction attempts one evening, I turned the conversation to his current writing and, upon learning that he needed to do research on Brownsville, offered to help. I asked Father to broker a meeting with

Jimmy, who knew everyone and every place in Brownsville. Jimmy then introduced us to Saul, one of the crime lords of the area.

Calling me "Sarah" all night because he couldn't remember my name, Saul drove us around the blight of Brownsville in his big white Cadillac. He packed a loaded gun as he walked us into pool halls and bars, obviously in charge of all that lay before him. Driving past a "Jesus Saves" sign over a building, he hissed an expletive and said, "See that! It used to be Temple Beth Israel."

Michael got his story thanks to Saul's introductions, and I arrived home at 3 a.m., shaken by the violent undercurrent of the night, worried about waking up on time for another day at the magazine. As promised, I called Father at that hour and, for the first time, he acknowledged his feelings about me when he sighed into the phone, "I was so worried about you. I thought you might have been killed."

Jimmy loved Father and admired his thinking. He defended Father to his fellow men of the cloth and was angry that they didn't support him too. One year after we were married, Jimmy arrived at our farmhouse in upstate New York with a woman friend, daughter of a powerful New York City judge. They were seeking our approval for their relationship. I fussed around the farmhouse before they arrived trying to be nonchalant about everything, making up beds in two different rooms, in case they weren't sleeping together and heading off to bed by myself on some excuse so as to not witness their choice of rooms. They married and had a child, Jimmy added law school to his credentials and began practicing law among the poor, continuing his priestly mission. We lost touch with them until Marge came to visit us a few years later to explain their distance from us. Sadly, Jimmy's alcohol and drug use kicked up mental illness. He deserted his family, fled to Chicago and went underground for many years, finally surfacing when he was at bottom. Another decade passed and we learned that Jimmy had divorced Marge and remarried and was running a successful law practice. He and Will had a great multiple-hour telephone conversation to catch up on their years apart. They promised each other to keep in touch but never did.

John

The handsome and elegant John almost always wore his professional garb, barely ever loosening his collar. He was a man with a future in the church. He and Father had traveled on vacation together, a surprising duo. Their last trip had been an extensive visit to the Middle East and Africa, which Father enjoyed no end. About two years after that, as we approached our wedding date, John took us to lunch at a trendy restaurant in Manhattan. I was impressed with his look and manner until he started telling me how much he disagreed with our plans for a life together and obviously disapproved of me. He handed me a generous check and without looking at me said sternly, "Take this. You know I can't agree with you and can't come to your wedding." The bizarre gesture terrified me. He brought back all those childhood fears of the man behind the screen in the confessional, the stern pastor, the unforgiving church. We left the restaurant, and I slumped on to the sidewalk, fainting as we hit the air outside.

Years later, when we visited John in his opulent rectory – he was a monsignor by then – I could only recall those feelings, never losing my fear of him. At the height of his priestly career he had a massive heart attack and died.

Tony

Tony was the one. He was the one who came to my apartment to get to know me, who bought a new suit for our wedding, not wanting to insult us by attending in his "clerics." He and Father worked in the Education Office of the diocese and enjoyed all sorts of arts events. They went to the beach. They loved to have a good time together. He didn't necessarily agree with Father's theological positions. Theology was never the issue. They were friends.

We three had the sweetest evening together when he made the special trip to my place for dinner four weeks before our wedding. His warm Italian personality enveloped me instantly, and I loved him for it. I have an eternal memory of him sinking comfortably into the green upholstered chair in my living room, smiling warmly, telling me of his large and loving family and how happy he was for Father's happiness.

Two weeks after our dinner and two weeks before our wedding Tony was found dead on a lonely street in New York. "Suspicious circumstances," said the *Daily News*. "Heart attack," said his family. We never knew. Father went to the wake and Tony's family, once loving and embracing to him, was cold and aloof. Not only had they lost their beloved brother and son, they were losing his also best friend William. Father never grieved Tony's death. He couldn't. It was too painful on the eve of marriage and too painful all the years since.

Joseph

Our first child was a newborn when Joe, Sully and Gus came to check us out. Joe was funny, friendly and distinguished by his beret, his beard, his love of beautiful liturgy. He was not quite able to disapprove of us because he loved Father and was, himself, questioning his priesthood. He left the active ministry at the age of 50 – after trying intensely to make the church work for him. During those years, he struggled – oh how he struggled – to remain a priest. It was psychoanalysis that helped him come to his decision to leave finally, after bearing the brunt of suffering and hysterical and violent threats from his widowed mother. While he had great sadness about leaving the priesthood, he had great joy in his beloved new wife and ultimately a rich and creative life. He always wanted to be a married priest. He and Will never agreed on that thinking. He lives a life centered on prayer and liturgy and is so very happily married for more than 25 years. He had become a social worker while in the priesthood, but when his creative self took over his life, he began a business that combined his artistic talent and his care for people. Joe and Will remained friends for a lifetime.

FAITH

In the Year of Our Lord, 1965

TRAVELS IN FASHION AND FAITH

This year – 1965 – was the year before we met. It was a year of tumult and excitement when events on the earth and in space were swirling with courageous adventures. Father and I were both on significant journeys in that year. The differences in those journeys make it even more remarkable to me that we came together. Maybe it was because of the differences that we did.

The March 1965 cover of *Harper's Bazaar* featured a Richard Avedon photograph of Jean Shrimpton, the British darling of the fashion world, peering from behind a bright day-glow pink space helmet with the magazine's logo vibrating against it in acid green. The *Time* magazine cover of March 19, 1965 featured a drawing of Martin Luther King Jr. and the cover story of the issue centered on the now violent national issue of the right to vote for all citizens.

On a January Monday in 1965, I embarked on the first leg of an historic cross-country trip designed to promote the new McDonnell Douglas DC-9 and Delta Airlines. My publisher had sold a multi-page advertising spread to the two companies to mark the launch of this twin-engine, single-aisle jet airliner, and he had arranged for a fashion house – Jerry Silverman Inc. – to design a collection to be featured in the magazine spread. The marketing promise was to attract fashion-conscious women to the clothing, to the aircraft and to flying.

Jet travel was still in its infancy. Business men primarily used short flights. Upscale leisure and business women travelers were a new and desirable market to be explored.

The DC-9 was special. Designed for frequent short flights, it became a most successful jet airliner, earning a reputation for reliability and efficiency. At its maximum it seated one hundred thirty-five passengers, creating a great theater for a comparatively intimate captive audience. The single aisle was important to this trip. It was going to be a fashion runway for my journey.

I believe it was the publisher who decided I was to be the magazine's representative on this junket. I guess now that because I was the youngest editor in the promotion department, I would be the best candidate for the rigors of the journey. Jerry Uchin, the Vice President of Silverman was a perfect companion for the trip. He was outgoing, pleasant and professional, guiding me that week through scenarios that were new and challenging.

It was still dark when I got out of bed. I hadn't slept very well in that single bed in that tiny bedroom of mine. It wasn't the bed that bothered me all night. It was excitement and anxiety about the upcoming journey. I lit my morning cigarette, put on a pot of coffee and shuffled into the shower. I always enjoyed that early morning routine, especially because the bathroom was bigger than my bedroom and I could run enough hot water to make it feel like a sauna.

Antonio had done my hair the night before, so I didn't have to fuss with that. His salon, on the first floor of my apartment townhouse, was fast becoming a *Bazaar* hangout. Since I had introduced him to the editorial staff and a few photographers, he was doing so much work at the magazine that I had gratis hairdos for a year.

I pulled the perfectly fitting dress over my head, carefully wiggling around so that I wouldn't mess up my hair. I had fashioned a scarf around the hairdo to wear while I was sleeping and then showering.

I had a week's wardrobe of Silverman designs to wear on the junket. It was just a matter of choosing one for the launch. Wanting to look grown up and serious and professional but chic, I chose a conservative black and white tweed outfit, a sleeveless, slim-skirted, belted dress with a waist-length tailored jacket. I was too excited to eat breakfast, even though my bags were packed and my apartment was so organized that Bernice would be able to clean during the week without spending her entire time picking up my stuff.

At 6:30 a.m., the driver arrived to take me to meet the entourage at Newark Airport. More time for smoking and enjoying coffee and chattering away with the driver to ease my nervousness. What was I afraid of? Flying, the weather, remembering my lines, maintaining my cool? I had spent weeks arranging everyone's itinerary, under the direction of the publisher and the Silverman, Douglas and Delta staffs who made all the high-level connections and the media contacts. Now the moment had come. All the prep work was behind me. I shifted my role from arrangements assistant to principal player.

We – three models, Jerry Uchin and I – gathered on the tarmac, meeting up with the airline executives. Cameras flashed as we posed on the steps of the aircraft. We left Newark, in the spotlight of the major New York City news media of the day, bound for Atlanta, the first stop on a week's adventure across the country. The big press conference would be held in Atlanta.

We were assigned VIP seats on the short flight. That was the last time for a week that we would be able to relax in public. We were background during the press conference, where the airline officials extolled the advantages of jet travel on short flights. Executives of Rich's department store were on hand. The upscale store would be promoting and selling the Silverman fashions as would other high-end stores in Memphis, Detroit, Chicago, San Francisco, New Orleans, Dallas, Miami and New York. And we were on our way to all of them.

After the press conference our aircraft headed down the Atlanta airport runway. As soon as we were safely airborne, we would begin a surprise, unannounced fashion show. There were at least five airline executives on board, anxious to greet passengers and gush about the new plane. Suddenly, we stopped on the runway. In spite of all the heavy corporate weight on board, the aircraft had blown a tire in Delta's hometown. Much hemming and hawing ensued until Delta decided to pour the Champagne while we were towed back to the gate. In a short time we were airborne again, the first of many adventuresome events behind us.

The five of us re-boarded the aircraft before the other passengers, giving us time to set up our event before they took their seats. No comfortable enclosed boarding passageway here. Everyone walked from the terminal across a short distance on the runway to mount the stairs to the plane. Jerry and I were stationed separately at the front and rear of the plane, slightly behind the flight attendants. Once the doors were locked and the passengers settled, the crew would begin serving drinks, no matter what time of the day. Most of the passengers were, of course, businessmen. Standing at the front of the plane I would examine their faces, musing about the stories behind those blank slates, wondering why they were on this journey.

The flight attendants, then known as stewardesses, were remarkably busy and always short of time. They were young, attractive, patient – ever so patient – hostesses who endured grumpiness, hostility, drunkenness, fear and sexual harassment with admirable professionalism. After serving drinks and with the finest choreography, they prepared meals in the kitchenettes located in the front of the plane. On our junket, they also had to make room for the models and the rack of fashions we were waiting to present.

As the passengers settled into their comfortable seats with their drinks and meals, I greeted them from the microphone at the front and introduced Jerry at the mike at the back of the plane while the stewardesses distributed the programs we had designed. We then began our fashion show. One by one the models sashayed down the aisle, chatting with the passengers, then returned to the kitchen area for a quick change. And did it again. All the while, Jerry and I were sharing the commentary from our separate mikes and I was also, with my left hand, helping un-zip, re-zip, pull off, put on, smooth down and push forward the next model. Some passengers, at first, seemed embarrassed or annoyed, only slyly glancing at the models in motion. Within a few minutes, however, most were enjoying the show. The tailored suit, topped with a wide-brimmed black hat that just skimmed the sides of the aisle, was, by far, the crowd pleaser of the collection. "Oh my gosh," one passenger exclaimed, sucking in his breath as the model Gail strutted by with that outrageous chapeau. The show lasted twenty minutes, just long enough so that we could get out of the way before the airplane was made ready for landing.

We managed to perform no matter the weather. Sometimes the models would be struggling in their high heels, mounting the aisle as the plane soared upwards or catching their bearings if turbulence hit, but they were pros and never missed a beat. It was only at the end of the week that they all started complaining about their sore feet and aching backs. And that was after doing fashion shows on ten flights followed by press conferences on the ground and more fashion shows and special dinners for VIP retail partners in each city. We had traveled Monday to Friday from Newark to Atlanta to Detroit, Memphis, Chicago and Denver, to San Francisco, Dallas, New Orleans, to Miami and home to Newark. Some days there were two shows, two press conferences and two retail events.

The clients were pleased with the extensive press coverage and the supportive response from the executives of Neiman Marcus, Burdines and Saks Fifth Avenue. Jerry and I had enjoyed each other's company. We took turns parenting the three models, who were all about ten years older than I, massaging their feet after a show, serving them tea, listening to their life stories, praising them, petting them, indulging them. We would have been lost without them, and while they generally were having an adventure, it was a very demanding week that in the 21st century, would probably be prohibited by a union contract.

Back at *Bazaar* late that Friday afternoon, I was welcomed with relief and cheers by the publisher and the promotion director. I was too fatigued to appreciate their applause. Reaching for my desk to pick up a paper, I was unable to touch the surface, feeling a little disoriented. After a few days of this weird feeling I met with the doctor and was diagnosed with a severe case of the newly identified condition called "jet lag."

After we had met in 1966, Father told me the following story:

A few weeks after my historic flight, on Thursday, March 25, 1965, Father Scanlan left LaGuardia Airport early, early in the morning, boarding a plane chartered by clergy of all faiths and bound for Montgomery, Alabama. Dressed in his clerical garb, he joined his two pals, Fathers Jim Regan and Charlie Cushing, officially suited up as well. He had asked Monsignor Eugene J. Molloy, his boss, the superintendent of the Education Office of the Brooklyn Diocese, for permission to be out of the office that day, explaining that he was going to join Martin Luther King Jr. on the last leg of the historic Selma to Montgomery march.

"I can't support what you're doing, but you can have the day off," was Monsignor's response. Disappointed, but not surprised, Father left the office and prepared for the early morning flight the next day.

The Brooklyn Catholic Church was not, in fact, supporting racial equality. Real estate was an important consideration. Diocesan leadership couldn't balance cash flow, its fear of white flight to the suburbs and redlining, and still appear to be supportive of black people.

The concerns of the office of the bishop were centered on maintaining the financial equilibrium of all the white parishes as well as the racial concerns of their parishioners.

Even though he was aware of the diocesan priorities, Father always preached equality among all people carefully, but firmly. He knew that he was not always in a friendly environment. In one Brooklyn neighborhood, a zealous priest, Father Barney Quinn, had established a black parish, St. Peter Clavier, in 1922. He did so because the pastor of an existing white parish, Father John Belford, refused to admit black people to worship. Forty years later it remained the only black parish in the diocese.

The flight to Montgomery was fully booked and filled with concerned clergy of all denominations. Father noticed the nervous bantering and gallows humor that went up and down the aisles, especially when they entered southern skies. "Are they starting to shoot at us yet?" one of the ministers joked. Years later, Father said to me. "This was all so serious for me. I was no longer just talking about racial inequality. I felt I was doing something about it."

He and his friends were joining twenty-five thousand people on the last leg of a historic civil rights march. As he explained to me later, the three Selma to Montgomery marches in 1965 were probably the emotional peak of the civil rights movement, sparked by the violent actions of Governor George Wallace and his minions against voting and all other civil rights for black people in Alabama. Wallace had denounced even a nonviolent march as a threat to public safety, declaring he would take all measures necessary to block the civil rights movement.

Media accounts documented the first march, on Sunday, March 7, 1965, which started on now-famous Alabama Highway 80. Led by John Lewis of the Student Nonviolent Coordinating Committee and Hosea Williams of the Southern Christian Leadership Conference, the

500 or so marchers walked only six blocks from Selma to the Edmund Pettus Bridge. At that spot, they were halted by state police in helmets and gas masks and the mounted sheriff's posse who brutally attacked with billy clubs, tear gas and bullwhips. Photographs of that violent scene appeared throughout the world on television, in newspapers and magazines, a scene so abusive that the event became known as Bloody Sunday.

In response to Bloody Sunday, Martin Luther King Jr. began organizing a second Selma to Montgomery march to be held two days later, on Tuesday, March 9, 1965. He called for people across the country to join him. This time, 2,500 marchers walked with Dr. King and the civil rights leaders but only as far as the Edmund Pettus Bridge, where Dr. King offered a short prayer. He then turned the marchers back to Selma so as not to violate the court order preventing them from marching all the way to Montgomery. That evening, three white ministers in the march were attacked and beaten with clubs by segregationists. Reverend James Reeb, a white Unitarian Universalist minister from Boston, was so severely beaten that he died a few days later in a Birmingham hospital.

A week after Reverend Reeb's death, the federal district court ruled in favor of the First Amendment right to protest, so that the state of Alabama could not block the march. Dr. King put out an appeal to clergy from all over the nation to join him in the non-violent walk to Montgomery. On March 21, 1965, 8,000 people assembled to begin the 55-mile trek from Selma to Montgomery. On March 22 and 23, the number of marchers was limited to 300 protestors most of whom were local black people. The other protesters who gathered were camped in muddy fields at the site of the City of St. Jude Hospital. The 36 acres of this, the first integrated hospital in the Southeast, had been offered to the marchers for rest and respite. On the morning of the 24th, the marchers crossed into Montgomery County and the highway widened into four lanes. All day, as the group approached the city, additional marchers were ferried by bus and car to join the line. By Thursday, March 25, 25,000 people marched from a campsite at the City of St. Jude, a Catholic complex on the outskirts of Montgomery, to the steps of the state Capitol.

Father and his two friends were led to the meeting place at the City of St. Jude. After disembarking from the plane in Montgomery that morning of the 25th, they were met by a sturdy young black man in overalls. He was dressed in what had become the symbolic uniform of the valiant black people of the South who were toiling in the movement for social and civil justice in the country. "Don't talk to anyone who is white," he stuttered. "Only ask questions of people who are dressed like me. We're the organizers and we're here all day and night to help you. It is too dangerous to talk to white people, so please don't do that."

Father remembered that stutter decades later. The young worker's affliction added solemnity to his message.

The three priests from Brooklyn joined the last leg of the journey, singing and walking for the rest of the day to the Alabama Capitol, surrounded by thousands of others. The words of "We Shall Overcome" and "This Little Light of Mine" were ones that Father would forever associate with this day. And the words of the stuttering worker rang in his ears as he passed the mocking, angry torments of the menacing crowds lining the route. Because of the court order, they couldn't touch the marchers. But they could spit on them and taunt them. Even though they were held back by local police and the National Guard, their hostile torments – "Yankee priest, go home" -- were very real and frightening, Father recalled to me years later, shuddering as he remembered.

Arriving at the Capitol, the marchers rallied to the inspirational words of Dr. King. His speech, "How Long, Not Long," praised "the pilgrimage of clergymen and laymen of every race and faith pouring into Selma to face danger at the side of its embattled Negroes." "Like an idea whose time has come," King continued, "not even the marching of mighty armies can halt us. We are moving to the land of freedom." Finally, he asked, "How long?" and answered, "Not long. Because the arm of the moral universe is long but it bends toward justice."

The priests from Brooklyn joyously prayed with their fellow clergy, inspired and strengthened by their witness in the midst of thousands, affirmed in their beliefs and at peace with their decision to be present. Late that same night, they returned to Brooklyn, physically unharmed and jubilant about the cause.

"I didn't know what I would do if I were arrested," Father later confessed. Still, he remained, for his entire life, exhilarated and unswerving in his decision to have been part of that monumental event.

LOVE

Love Story

ALIA JACTA SUNT
A Game of Chance

The priest was playing bridge with her that afternoon as the Mamas and Papas singing "California Dreaming" drifted across the boardwalk in front of her cabana. Mary, Father and the O'Connors, an easy-going, friendly and comfortable Irish Catholic couple, were gathered for their weekly summer game. They had all met a few years earlier at this, their summer haven, the Atlantic Beach Club. Situated on a beautiful strip of land between the ocean and the Long Island Sound, the "Christian Club," as it was known, was enjoyed by middle class Catholics and Protestants from Queens and Long Island.

Father Scanlan rented a cabana every summer, primarily for the pleasure of his parents. He'd meet them on Sunday afternoon, after Mass. He and his father and mother, sometimes joined by a nephew or two, swam and played cards, catching up on family affairs while they enjoyed dinner together in the clubhouse before heading home Sunday night, refreshed from the gifts of the Long Island Sound.

Mary also rented a cabana there every summer. It was a refuge from her large, beautiful and troubled home a few miles away. She was thirty-eight years old that summer of 1966. She and her six children – Michael, Imogene, William, Samuel, Elizabeth and Thomas, toddler to teenagers – spent weekends, safe from her husband and distracted from her reality. Her cabana was directly across the strip of sand from the priest's. Station wagon unpacked with the food and drinks for her brood and their many friends, she and the kids marched to the cabana with the help of one of the cabana boys, where she plunked the food in the kitchenette and organized the children's clothing for the day, along with diapers, first aid equipment, books and games. After dousing everyone with suntan lotion and sending them off to a swimming class or to play with friends, she put one of her favorite 45's on the record player, grabbed a book and settled into the lounge chair in front of the cabana, sunglasses and hat on, a different bathing suit flattering her body each day. She was trim, attractive and energetic. She was cheerful and kind despite her troubled marriage. She was also strict with the children as a quasi-single mother must be.

My cousin Mary and I were very close, despite our twelve years age difference. Not only did we share a first name, we also shared similar views on life. She and her sister, Nanci, had been raised by our grandparents. Their mother, Imogene, suffered from schizophrenia. She was institutionalized for life in a Pennsylvania state hospital, never to be seen or heard of again. Her husband, Bill McDonald, my mother's oldest brother, was a successful businessman and a rogue, and not capable of raising his two young girls alone. So they lived with our grandparents from the time their mother was committed until their teens when their father remarried and took them to live with him and his new wife. He and Kata were married in a civil ceremony, not able to have a Catholic wedding, according to church law, because his first wife, even though institutionalized for life, was still alive. Bill had divorced her, but church law forbade him to marry another while she was still alive. Kata was widowed with four children, a warm and happy woman with a generous smile, a huge bosom and a deep-throated hearty laugh. She created a rich and loving home, nurturing Mary and Nanci and their four step-siblings.

Bill and Kata's marriage outside the church was scandalous to some. But no one could help but love Kata. Everyone was so relieved that Bill had finally settled down in his forties, relieved that Mary and Nanci were with their dad, that our grandparents, now in their seventies, were no longer saddled with their care.

Everyone, that is, except my mother. She stopped speaking to Bill when he married Kata, merely nodded to them at family gatherings and spoke to Kata again only after Bill died some twenty years later. He was a sinner in the eyes of the church. My mother would not speak to a sinner.

The O'Connors' cabana was next to Mary's. They found the comings and goings of Mary and her brood amusing and wonderful, although they worried about her being alone all the time. She told them half the truth – that her husband (whom she had married when she was nineteen) was in the restaurant business and couldn't get away on weekends. Of course, during the season, he was also at the racetrack. They accepted that explanation and included her in their activities.

They all loved playing bridge, as long as no one took it seriously. Mary welcomed any intellectual challenge and thrived on competition. One Sunday when one of their usual foursome couldn't join them, Tom O'Connor suggested they invite the priest from across the boardwalk. "He seems like a nice fellow," Tom said, "and he'll certainly be harmless for you, Mary." She agreed with a laugh, and Tom extended the invitation. The priest accepted it happily, confessing that he wasn't a very good bridge player but welcomed their company. They all assured him they weren't either. "This is only a game of chance," Mary said, letting him know it was not to be taken too seriously. Thus began a bridge foursome that lasted for years.

Father never knew many of the details of Mary's life, although he knew that there was trouble with her marriage. After saying all the Sunday Masses he had agreed to take on, he preferred to be "off duty," so he never got into serious personal conversations with her. He knew that she and the kids were always at the club on weekends until closing time. Her husband was nowhere to be seen. Father did meet him once at some event (later he couldn't remember what it was) and was impressed with what he thought was a handsome, charming man. What he didn't know until a few years after that was how the same guy was also a gambler and a philanderer who abused his wife and was reputedly affiliated with the mob. His gambling became so excessive that the successful business that his father built and entrusted to his son was in shambles.

Father was very careful around Mary, afraid that any personal comments might be misconstrued, careful never to be alone with this attractive woman. *Numquan solus cum sola.* He tried to meet her only when all four of them were at the bridge table. By chance one afternoon, as they were casually talking during a hand, he mentioned to his bridge pals that he had a problem.

"The editor of my doctoral thesis, this priest named Gennaro D'Ecclesiis, is leaving for Italy," he said. "I'm really going to need another editor. My chairman says I can't write, and I have to get this thing finished soon. Any of you know anyone who can help me?"

Mary spoke up, "I have a cousin works at *Harper's Bazaar*. She does freelance work. Would you like me to call her?"

Father was relieved and excited, asking Mary to call me as soon as she could. He also asked for my phone number. The next day, Mary called to let me know "this guy, a priest from the beach club, is going to call you to see if you want to edit his thesis." I was delighted. The timing couldn't have been better. I needed all the extra work I could get to support the single girl in the city lifestyle I had chosen. The priest's project sounded more challenging than writing copy and creating style names for a shoe catalogue, one of my regular freelance jobs. I told Mary to give the priest permission to call me, which he did the next night.

"I'm looking for an editor for my work," he said. "And I have a deadline. Could we meet next week and talk about my dissertation?" Pretending to be terribly busy, I agreed to meet for lunch the following week, on July 14, 1966. "Bring a couple of chapters with you," I instructed him with great bravado, "and I'll see if I can work it into my schedule."

INTROIT

I happily left my office around noon on that sweltering Bastille Day in 1966, glad to be escaping the dirty and hot old building that housed the chic lifestyle magazines of the Hearst Corporation. I was feeling curious, secretive and a just a little bit giddy, and steeled by a dose of cynicism that I had adopted towards anyone or anything Catholic.

"Here I am meeting this Catholic priest for lunch," I told myself for the millionth time "How ironic." The walk gave me the time I needed to momentarily temper the passion of my struggles with Catholicism. Since I was nineteen years old, my relationship with the church had been growing and regressing between fascination with its history, enraged at its attitude towards and treatment of women, love of its mystery and liturgy, especially music, and shame about being a member of an archaic, paternalistic corporation. I was increasingly suspicious of the social justice movement that seemed to be a cover-up for evangelism and then ashamed of my cynical attitude towards the wonderful work of some of the people of the church. It confused me that I could mock the culture that deified figures like Bishop Sheen and popular saints and still be attracted to prayer and good works. For five years I tossed from rage to fear, to fury and loneliness, to isolation and self-doubt, to romantic memories and longing, back to rage and then to wavering about my convictions.

Walking across 59th Street from 56th Street and Madison Avenue, rushing in the heat and humidity so as not to be late, was also a challenge to my appearance, especially to the condition of my B.H. Wragge designer black-linen suit topped with a yellow silk scarf. In the morning as I was getting ready for work, I thought, "Whatever I wear, I have to preserve some image of order in the midst of excitement." I reasoned it had to be something sophisticated and slightly serious, protective coloring against my immaturity and anxiety. My feet were shod in the most chic and uncomfortable pointy-toed Italian shoes and I was careful to preserve balance in my stride, especially up and down stairs.

I was meeting Father Scanlan at the New York Athletic Club on 59th Street and Central Park South, a hearty six- or seven-block walk. An avid squash player, he had been a member of the club for a few years.

The streets around the park have been romantic backdrops for me since I drooled over ice cream at Rumpelmayers. As children we joyously rode the carousel on special Sundays, skated on the pond in winter, visited the zoo ("Come see your relatives in the monkey house," Dad always joked) and fed the horses resting along the park's edge.

Approaching the New York Athletic Club I teetered slightly on the stone stairs leading to the main hall of the club. At the end of the corridor, a smiling man was energetically headed towards me with a thick file of papers under his arm. All the right clues were there for me to know immediately that he was the reverend I was to meet. He was in his official attire of black suit a white clerical collar, he clearly recognized me, and he was on time. He enthusiastically and most politely ushered me into the club's formal, white table-clothed, members-only dining room where we sat at a table overlooking Central Park. I ordered cold salmon with sauce vert from the terrible serious waiter.

"I expected a *Harper's Bazaar* editor to be an older lady in a flowered dress and wearing a big hat," he confessed somewhat shyly. We self-consciously laughed over that vision, and I noticed his beautiful blue eyes behind black-rimmed glasses – clear blue eyes, rimmed by hearty eyebrows. He had a nice, small nose and a slightly crooked smile that displayed a baby tooth where an adult one should have been. Brown curly hair was obviously kept under control by a short buzz cut. He didn't seem uncomfortable, although I thought his enthusiasm was beyond real and probably a sign of something. I wasn't sure what that was. Certainly, he looked like the movie-star classic handsome priest with his trim physique, kept that way, I later learned, by regular games of squash at the club and careful eating. But his behavior and his response to issues were so modern, and so similar to mine. That meeting of the minds was the start of the chemistry between us.

After a few personal exchanges, we moved on to business, discussing his doctoral thesis. Father told me he was keen on completing his degree as soon as possible. I wasn't sure why he was so intent about his deadline. Without ever checking my credentials, relying solely on the reference from my cousin and without taking a note, he asked me to consider becoming his editor. The hour we had planned ran on to almost two.

Even though I knew that day that I wanted to do the work, I demurred on instant commitment. I was going on vacation with my dear friend and confidant Nancy and knew I needed to discuss this with her. Father gave me the first three chapters to review while I was away. We agreed that I would get back to him in two weeks with a response. He offered me a fee of $50 a chapter. In 1966 that seemed like a fair and respectful amount, especially given the $75 weekly salary I was making at the famous fashion magazine.

Friendly, a little awkward and excited, we walked out of the club after lunch, down those main stairs and onto the steaming street. I was now late getting back to the office and my feet were finished walking the streets for the day, so I was prepared to take a cab back to my office. But Father offered me a ride. Crossing the beautifully expansive street, we arrived at his parked Volkswagen Beetle. He invited me to get into the back seat of the car. When I offered both surprise and objection, he explained that he had a policy. "I don't allow women to sit in the front seat of my car," he said. His rule even included his mother, he told me, who, I discovered later, always rode regally on the right side of the back seat.

Trying not to show my disdain for the rule, I demurred from the back seat ride, saying, "Thanks, but I'll enjoy walking back to my office."

In a swift moment, Father removed all the stuff piled up on the passenger seat and sheepishly invited me to take the front seat. We drove the short route engaging in stilted conversation until we got to Madison Avenue and 57th Street. As I reluctantly climbed out of the car, I promised to contact him about his proposal when I returned from vacation.

Over the next two weeks, I spent little time considering whether I would work on Father's thesis, consulting with my dear friend as we cycled around the beach towns of Cape Cod. I knew almost immediately after the lunch meeting that I would take on the job. Not only could I use the extra money, I was also excited to have an intellectual challenge to supplement my stimulating and difficult but non-intellectual work at *Harper's Bazaar*.

I called Father when I returned from vacation, saying, "I'll be happy to take on the work, but we have to make a plan so that we can meet your deadline." We made a very professional arrangement, agreeing that I would take the subway from Madison Avenue to Brooklyn every Wednesday after work. We would meet at his rectory at 6 p.m. and work for three hours, and he would get me a cab home to Manhattan.

Father had no idea that I was terrified of subways. Years of traveling to and from high school in those dark, dank tunnels, encountering that unwelcome vile stalker, had left their mark on me. But this ride to Brooklyn was a relatively short and uncrowded, so I could endure it. At the station nearest his rectory, where the train elevated from the tunnel to street level, Father met me at the bottom of the subway staircase and drove me – in the front seat – to the rectory.

After a few weeks, Father decided that my cab ride back to Manhattan after our work was too much for me. "I'll drive you home," he said, worried, he claimed, that I was being worn out by long and complicated days. I was worn out, but also exhilarated by our work together.

I should have known when I first saw his car that there was something different about this priest. Unlike his colleagues who drove black Chryslers or Fords or, worse yet, Cadillacs, he drove a gray Volkswagen. I could tell he enjoyed the image of himself in a gray off-color proletarian auto.

There was always a "Clergy" sign on the right side of the dashboard, which came in handy a few times when we were either parked in a no-parking zone or driving over the speed limit. The cop on Northern Boulevard in Queens who stopped Father one evening was in a dilemma when, after a sarcastic comment and while preparing the speeding ticket, asked for his driver's license. Next to him, I giggled nervously. Looking at the license, the cop realized he had stopped a priest in civilian clothes with a woman next to him, driving too fast on that busy thoroughfare. In 1967 that was a rare sight. Embarrassed and confused, the cop said, "Oh never mind, Father. Just drive more carefully." Will asked for the ticket, but it was already torn up.

That vehicle became a safe haven for us, the only place where we initially talked about things that really mattered to us. In the rectory we would discuss ideas about the Catholic Church, about religion and politics. We would argue over the content or format of his dissertation, "The Development of the American Catholic Diocesan Board of

Education, 1884-1966." Those discussions were important as we grew to know each other's political leanings and tested each other's brainpower. It was the deep and intimate conversation in the car as we crossed the bridge to Manhattan and parked near my nest that topped off each meeting.

As the months progressed, time in the car became precious. We began to reveal the depths of our selves, effortlessly the way old friends or soul mates do.

Intimacy began in that car, not with the usual romantic scene of backseat groping and explorations, but in the front seat with intense, intellectual discourse. We talked about our ideas of God, about the early failures of Vatican II. We agonized over the civil rights struggles we were living through. We tackled feminism as that issue became an increasingly important and controversial topic. Eerily enough, we agreed, with some minor hiccups, on all the things that mattered to each of us.

If we kept to our plan as we devised it and met and worked every Wednesday, the thesis could be presented in six months. That would give Father time to make whatever changes his committee requested and assure him that he would be awarded his doctoral degree in May 1967. As much as Father was keen and determined about that deadline, he was also very keen and determined that we meet and work in a safe and appropriate place. And I took his determination seriously.

AD ALTARE DEI

The day usually began with a Pall Mall – or two, if truth be told – and a couple of cups of coffee. My ten-block New York City stride to the fashion magazine office was always energizing and purposeful and exciting. Interesting people and sights were a daily delight. I would leave the little townhouse, running down the marble steps, wrestling open the heavy brass front door polished lovingly each day by Manuel the super. There were only six floors in the narrow 1920s building, with two tenants to a floor above the elegant retail on the first two floors. In true New York tradition, the tenants were unknown to each other.

Days were often frantic – deadlines driving work, moods, relationships, creativity and power. But then there was lunch in a trendy setting with a glamour queen or a man of power or at the counter at Henry Halper's Drugstore on the street floor of the building, a tuna fish sandwich with an egg cream next to the likes of Anthony Quinn and other stars who would drop in for lunch and hope not to be noticed. (Of course, even though my heart pounded sitting next to Quinn, who I assumed must have lived in the neighborhood, I never acknowledged his presence except to nod my head when I left the counter.) At the very least, I and other young editorial assistants ate deli sandwiches at our desks, in the splendor of sooty papers. In those days, all New York City buildings without air conditioning were sooty in the summer when the windows had to be opened and dusty in winter with closed windows and steam heating.

When luncheon was elegant, it was very elegant, often at eateries of the moment – La Caravelle, Cote Basque or La Grenouille – with a senior editor, a designer, a manufacturer or a retail merchant. Sometimes it occurred in the lounge at the St. Regis Hotel with my director from the fashion magazine, on her expense account. We regularly met in an undiscovered corner of the hotel, creating promotion plans for the magazine and gossiping about the personalities and people we had to deal with every day. At these monthly meetings we were often treated to the appearance of Salvador Dali strolling by in his red-satin lined cape and with his walking stick, searching for dames and admiring glances from the world. He always nodded at us. "Ladies, good afternoon," he would say with a flourish as he bowed slightly. We were thrilled each time.

Dinner was often skipped in the interest of being thin or because of limited funds. A good date was the man who bought you dinner during an evening and then took you home and left you at the door without a wrestle.

On the days that I went to the rectory in Brooklyn, there was no time for food between the *Harper's Bazaar* day and the Brooklyn evening. Usually I left the office without disclosing to anyone where I was going, boarding the E train at 57th street, which crossed under the river to Queens, getting off at Ely Avenue at 21st Street in Long Island City. It was a bit of a squeamish ride, watching out for the stalker, worrying about being trapped in a tunnel under the river. I made the journey once a week that year. It was a confusing return to a reality I thought was behind me.

Father would greet me joyfully, and we would take the short trip in his gray Beetle to the rectory where he lived with five other priests. Our destination neighborhood was working class, gray and a little grimy. A few puny New York trees, litter in the gutters, tin cans and other detritus scattered about in lots. Kids, the sons and daughters of Polish, Italian, German and Irish immigrants, played stickball in the alleys around the church. Old men and women, people from these native countries, prayed in the dark pews.

As we drove there that first day, Father told me that the ministry of St. Cecilia's, his parish, was to the many immigrants and first-generation Catholics of Greenpoint who were not Polish. The Polish Catholics had their own church and school. The parishioners of his church unloaded cargo at the Brooklyn docks, labored in the Eberhard-Faber Pencil factory, the electrical manufacturing plant in the community, the lumberyards or the meatpacking company. Facing the East River, the residents of Greenpoint could sit in McCarren Park and gaze at Manhattan, lit on a summer evening by the searchlight from the Empire State Building. This was a community that worked hard, played hard and prayed hard.

"Let me show you around the place," Father said when we first arrived at the old church buildings. Whirling around, as I discovered was a habit of his, he found all the keys he needed and began the tour. I felt very special when I was taken to the inner workings of the sacristy. It was not a place where women often visited, unless they were washing and ironing altar linens or priest vestments. Father proudly showed me the varieties of vestments carefully stored in long wooden drawers, explaining the other liturgical accessories kept in the sacristy. He walked me around the room pointing out the traditions and workings of the sacristy and then showed me the ritual of dressing for Mass. The sacristy flanked the sanctuary of the old parish church. The walls were lined with dark oak cupboards with long drawers, rather like an artist's flat file. The sacristy on one side of the altar was reserved for the priests. The other side was for the use of altar boys, parish volunteer workers and church societies.

The Altar Rosary Society ladies were there every week, with their hats on of course, to pick up or return the altar linens they had lovingly washed and ironed for the priests. Even though they were about to do housekeeping work, they wore dresses or suits that were not quite their Sunday best. These extraordinarily dedicated women prayed the rosary in unison each week at their meeting and took care of the altars, cleaning the marble, polishing the wood, brass and silver, laundering the linens in their homes, refreshing the flowers, doing all the non-sacramental duties that needed to be done for the priests.

These ladies were one notch down on the ladder to heaven of Catholic women's groups, just under the Arch Confraternity of the Mothers of Priests, it was believed. That confraternity, to which my future mother-in-law belonged, was really special in the days when priesthood was considered really special. More than 20 years after Will and I were married, her son's ordination photo fell out of my mother-in-law's wallet when I was helping her find her health insurance card at a doctor's office. She sheepishly smiled when I asked her what the ordination photo was doing in her wallet years later. "Once the Mother of a Priest, always the Mother of a Priest," she confessed. There was an assumption among Catholics of the 1940s and '50s that the men who became priests did so because they came from splendid mothers who prayed for their priesthoods and their own souls, winning victory in both cases when their sons became priests. I don't know what ever happened to the fathers of priests.

Alone or in the midst of altar boys, vesting for the liturgy was a ritual in itself. Father then showed me how he prepared for Mass, reverently kissing each Eucharistic vestment as he donned it and then prayed. He wore his uniform of black pants, white Roman collar and black cassock during the day. But for liturgy there was a big ritual. First on was the amice, a white linen shawl with strings hanging from the hem. After kissing it, Father pulled it over his head, settled it on his shoulders, said some prayers in Latin and tied it around his waist. Next on was the alb, a long white gown, like a big white nightgown, long sleeved, completely covering the body to the ankles, also made of linen. They were one-sized, hung like ghost robes in a closet in the sacristy, for each priest to use as he needed. The alb was tied with a white cincture, a twined fabric belt girding the priest with the promise of chastity. As each layer was added there was a prayer. Once the alb was tied, Father kissed the maniple, a symbolic handkerchief, and pinned it to his left arm. He reverently and prayerfully laid the stole across his shoulders. A priest crossed both sides of the stole over his breast, tucking it into the cincture. A deacon had to fling one side of the stole over his shoulder. A bishop left both sides hanging down at his side. Finally, before leading the altar boys to the sanctuary to say the Mass, the priest slipped the chasuble – an ornate little house – over his body. It and the maniple and stole would be of the same color, determined by the liturgical season or feast – red for a martyr's feast, white for a virgin, gold for high holy days. Fully adorned, the priest was ready to celebrate the Mass. Afterwards, the priest returned to the sacristy and removed his vestments with the same attention and devotion, handing each piece to an altar boy to be stored properly for the next liturgy.

After this wonderfully informative demonstration, we moved from the sacristy to the rectory, a Victorian brownstone built, no doubt lovingly, by the blue-collar parishioners – the immigrants who landed here in the 19th century into the comforting arms of Mother Church on the edge of Brooklyn. I couldn't help thinking of those people who labored in what I was now thinking of as a very suspicious organization which exploited women, facilitated some strange behaviors in its priestly work force and was just then, in 1966, rolling back the clock on so many personal issues deeply affecting its loyal members.

The dining room of the rectory was a large rectangular room of heavy, ornate and dulled dark furniture. In the center of the room was a long table that seated twelve – surrounded by chairs and covered neatly with a white damask cloth. Silver napkin rings of various shapes lay on the table, each marked with its owner's initials. With the exception of that one night when I was a special guest, I never saw anyone dine in that room.

From the first I was struck by the complete lack of sexism in this man. At the time I was still dating different men, learning my social/ sexual likes and dislikes, happy to be on my own as a single woman. I was in no hurry to get married, not envious of my college friends who had done so immediately or soon on after we graduated. Dad fretted a little over my single status, especially after my sister Alice married. Even though he had always encouraged me to do whatever I wanted to do professionally, he was beginning to question me about my social life, looking for the eligible prospect.

Since at first, Will was "Father," I told him everything about my social life. He expressed interest in my dating life, and I revealed many details to him, assuming he was a safe confidant. I was frank with him about my personal feelings about the Catholic Church, sensing from the beginning there was something different about this priest, which gave me the courage to discuss with him my deep and disturbing anger at the church. As our conversations became more intimate, we found that we had come to the same conclusions about our religious beliefs although at different times in our lives and on different paths.

Since Will was twelve years older than I, we had different reference points. Of course, his education in the priesthood had been vastly different from my education at Catholic schools and then a liberal college and graduate school. But we had both come to believe that the church was not serving us well, was not serving its members well and was, in fact, repressive and damaging to believers. I was angry about it. He was not. But he was ready to seriously confront his role as a member of the faith.

He was a successful priest, a kind of vice president of a powerful institution. He worked with enthusiasm, intensity, high intelligence and great, whimsical humor. It was expected that he would go far in the church hierarchy. He was responsible, successfully running a major division and never causing any embarrassment to the corporation. His staff was loyal to him, in even his darkest days when they faced possible conflict with their institutional loyalty.

Author Robert Timberg was a member of Father's first parish, a great athlete and all-around good and happy kid. He went on to become a distinguished graduate of the U.S. Naval Academy, a journalist at the *Baltimore Sun* and an author of a number of books, including a biography of John McCain. His book, "State of Grace," captures life on the threshold of the American Camelot, before the Beatles, before the pill, before Vatican II and before the shadow of the Vietnam War and the social and civil rights upheavals of the '60s.

He wrote the following about Father in "State of Grace": "My church, Queen of Peace, held confessions on Saturdays from 4 to 6 and 7:30 to 9, though you have to wonder why the confessionals didn't run twenty-four hours a day and have a hotline to boot considering the consequences of dying with a mortal sin on your soul. Usually two priests, sometimes three, manned the confessionals. You maneuvered to get the best priest, meaning the one who got you in and out as quickly as possible, thus precluding any detailed discussion of your sins. I always tried to get Father Scanlan, a young priest who had baptized me, taught me catechism and prepared me for my first Holy Communion and Confirmation. Because Father Scanlan didn't ask questions – just listened, then assigned penance – he was very popular with the teenage crowd, which led to jammed pews outside his confessional. If you were on a tight schedule, you'd have to take your chances with one of the other priests, which could be dicey.

There were always a lot of teenagers at confession. I assumed the girls were there as a social thing because what could they have to confess? The guys, I figured, probably had taken the Lord's name in vain, maybe lapsed into a morose delectation or two. I knew I was the worst, unless there was a murderer in our midst. Sometimes someone would go into the confessional and be in there as long as ten minutes. As he or she emerged, my friends and I would exchange nervous glances, decided we need to stretch our legs, casually drift back to Father Scanlan's line."

These were days of innocence, when Father was filled with the spirit of the church, enthusiastically working with his parishioners to help them live their lives. Part of that work was the weekly confession assignment. Catholics were encouraged to go to confession every week as a healthy spiritual practice. They had to go to confession if they wanted to receive Holy Communion and had committed a mortal sin. Mortal sins ranged from murder to intentionally eating meat on Friday. Venial sins – the less serious – included run-of-the-mill human errors like cursing, anger and disobedience to parents. A Catholic could partake of Holy Communion with a venial sin, although it could be an uncomfortable spiritual state for scrupulous believers.

Father entered the confessional center doors on Saturday afternoons and evenings, book and breviary in hand, picked his stole off the hook and arranged his cassock over his black slacks as he sat down on the upholstered chair in the dark wood confessional box He always also brought a book in case there was a break in the action. When he switched on the light, the first penitent on line outside the box knew it was time to enter and kneel in one of the side cubbies. Another penitent, on the line that formed on the opposite side of the box, would enter the other side, kneel and wait his turn. Father would slide open the screen separating him from each penitent and begin the ritual. For the next few hours, he listened to curiously unimaginative reports of events that people needed to get off their chests. Once a penitent expressed sorrow and a firm purpose of amendment, Father would assign a penance, usually prayer, offer absolution with the sacramental powers bestowed on him at ordination. That meant that the sinner was cleansed from sin once absolved and agreeing to perform the penance. For Father, hearing confessions every week while he was a parish priest was a tedious routine. "Anyone who has ever done this knows," he divulged, "It's like sitting in a closet."

THE VISITS OF THE MAGI

We carefully and respectfully folded back the white damask cloth on the dining room table and settled into our work. Father positioned himself at the head of the table, and I sat at his left, intensely reading, reviewing, challenging each other's thinking. As we prepared Father's doctoral dissertation, a huge document, full of quotations and tables and footnotes in Latin and English that needed to be perfectly recorded in the university's archaic academic formulae. During our three hours together, we seemed to discuss each sentence, each thought, each paragraph with passion.

The atmosphere in the dining room of the stodgy old rectory was vibrant while we were working. Thoughts raced out of control through my head. Why am I so comfortable with this untouchable man whom I have only known for a few weeks? How can I work with him and not flirt with him? I certainly think he's attractive. How can I even consider flirting with him! How can I keep the distance dictated by Mother Church? Why doesn't he seem to worry about distance while keeping his distance?

Father maintained physical space from me so naturally that it didn't occur to me that he had years of practice. How could he be so intimate and so self-contained? Why was he so at ease with himself when I was so internally frazzled? I'm probably just enjoying the intellectual challenge that doesn't exist at the fashion magazine, I reasoned. But then, working for a fashion magazine, I always argued, was really a philosophical study in aesthetics. Fashion was all about beauty, wasn't it?

During our working evenings, Father's rectory mates would drop into the dining room. A curious parade of men, they invariably offered me sweets, drinks, conversation and comments. Searching for something, never asking the question. I had no idea why they kept visiting us. They arrived in formal black cassocks with clerical collars, in give-away black pants with polo shirts, greenish-brown polyester golf shirts and slacks, their garments as pretentious or as understated as their personalities.

Maybe they made the procession to our place of work, I told myself, because the dining room was the center of community for this group of five. In fact, eating was their only earthly community. And eat they did, with passionate appetites. Father once told the story about the night they, as a community ritual, devoured an entire chocolate cake without thought. He mused that they were probably relishing the chocolate as a substitute for sex.

Culinary arts in the rectory were presided over by women – usually members of the parish or relatives of the pastor. After a few months, when my presence in their midst became more of a ritual, Father invited me to join him and his fellow priests for dinner one evening. I eagerly, although with some timidity, attended, curious to learn more about the celibate religious world Father inhabited. From the beginning of the long and luxurious meal, I knew I was the object of much speculation, especially by Mary, the cook. She was a solidly built Italian-American, middle-aged woman with a prominent chest that she bore proudly while carrying trays laden with an excess of food. As she processed into the room with her gifts, she gave me a sidelong sneer that sent shivers through my body. Of course, I could hardly eat but was in awe of the abundance of rich food and drink.

Although they were living in a house like family, as Father explained to me, the priests lived their lives and performed their daily duties very separately – saying Mass, hearing confessions, counseling families, managing the finances of the parish, reciting their ritual prayers alone, presiding over parish organizations and schools. Each had his own bedroom, his own sacred metaphorical sanctuary.

The pastor of the church was an older American Irishman, kind and gentle. If he were not a priest, he could have been a responsible, bland, mild-mannered and good husband and father. I could see him in an innocuous middle-management position in an insurance company. No one would ever know what was in his heart.

The other priests included a pious, not to say zealous man with absolutely no sense of humor and a narrow intelligence. There was also an older Italian-American, a career priest, not interested at all in progress in the church, just doing his job. Then there was the recovering alcoholic, another unenlightened man, consumed with staying in the priesthood, his ticket to heaven. No longer drinking alcohol, he prayed a lot. Lastly, there was a younger hip priest in his first parish assignment who was very involved in the more socially advanced movements in the church of the '60s and who became more and more engaged with us in conversation.

Each week, I met them all. Why did they keep interrupting us? Didn't they know we had work to do, that we had a deadline, that this was important? Each visit was a conundrum to me, especially since they asked the same questions week after week, parading in one by one over the three hours, bearing their small offerings. Father didn't seem to notice them too much nor did he explain to me why they kept coming into the dining room. At first, I thought they were sweet and solicitous. After a few months, I found them annoying and intrusive. They were patronizing, overly zealous in their attention to me. It never occurred to me that they were monitoring me and suspiciously watching the interaction between Father and me.

"We need to change this," I said after a few months. "We have a deadline. We can't endure this constant visiting," I huffed. One evening, it seemed perfectly natural for me to suggest that, in the future, we do our work at my apartment in Manhattan. The suggestion just fell out of my mouth without planning or conscious forethought. Working at my place would save me the travel time and we could focus, I said.

Father agreed but said he would set up the standards for work in this new environment and would let me know what we needed to do. "Of course," I agreed, knowing that we had to continue to be professional. There was no question. I had the solution. We could work as we had in the dining room – without the visits of the Magi.

LOVE

More Love

MANHATTAN AGGIORNAMENTO

On a winter night early in 1967, Father secretly came to my apartment, as we had planned, to continue the work in front of us. Dressed in chinos and a red and white striped shirt, he stepped, for the first time, into the little entryway to my flat, so little that it was often the scene of an awkward wrestling match between me and a date at the end of an evening. But this was not a date. I wanted to greet him with a hug, partly to assure both of us that everything was just fine and no one needed to be nervous. I was a wreck. I really didn't know what to do with this untouchable man.

"I can't hug him," I told myself. That would be unthinkable. I stepped aside, backing unexpectedly into the closet behind me in order to let him pass me and head into the living room. My heart was in havoc as I greeted him, formally, as my client and professional colleague. Without speaking we knew that our lives were dramatically changing.

Before that first night, I had shyly asked Father if he'd have dinner with me before we started working. He agreed, and I spent hours fretting over what to fix for dinner before deciding to make something that would appear utterly simple.

It was a most memorable lamb chops and spinach salad feast, which he enjoyed and I could barely touch. After the meal he asked, "What was that delicious meat?" When I told him, he said, "I always thought I didn't like lamb."

My typewriter rested on grandmother's table that doubled as my dining table. I cleared the dishes and returned the typewriter to its home, ready to make changes and additions to the text. He didn't dare move from the sofa that evening, but I was sure I could feel his breath from across the room. Our initial restraint was admirable, doomed to failure. Nevertheless we tried.

The focal point of my living room was a fireplace, which I framed with a traditional arrangement of sofa, coffee table, chair and hassock. That was about all the furniture I could afford. I created an eating area at one end of the room, using the best piece of furniture in the place, my grandmother's drop leaf mahogany table. I had decided before Father arrived that that could be our workspace. At the far end of the living room were two almost floor-to-ceiling windows that led to an urban patio. The only issue with the windows was that in order to get to that patio, you had to climb up and out of them. Off the living room were a large bathroom and a kitchen so small that when the oven door was opened, the cook had to step out into the living room. Also off the living room was my Lilliputian bedroom that could only hold a twin-sized bed and a night table and lamp. The bedroom closet was a tiny step-up arrangement crammed with my clothing.

On that first winter night in my nest, Father had an opening speech to make.

Striding into the living room, he said, "We have some serious boundaries to maintain." With that Father set about establishing those boundaries. He immediately walked over and firmly closed the door to the bedroom. Then, planting himself squarely in the middle of the living room as if he owned it, he declared, "The coffee table is our bundling board. You pick your side and stay there, and I'll stay on the other side." I blushed and giggled at his reference to the 18th century custom of sharing a bed with a special board between courting couples to prevent intimacy. In deference to his status as a guest, I offered him the sofa while I sat on the other side of the pathetic coffee table, in the cozy green chair with its hassock. "No one is to cross to the other's side of the table," he pronounced. I agreed without questioning. We were not to continue the intimate conversations of the car once we left it. The apartment was a workplace.

"Furthermore," he stated, "we have that immovable deadline, and we still have some serious content issues to work on." This dissertation had to be done in a few months. His self-imposed rule was to write a page a day. He often wrote more. I had to edit those pages every week, adding complicated footnotes, checking facts and ensuring the text's consistent style. I made arrangements with a young graphic artist from the magazine to create the charts and graphs Father wanted to include in the manuscripts. These would add depth and interest to the text. The thesis came alive and we saw an ending. However, we persevered in the face of more important work, discussing, changing, adding, removing, arguing, refining thoughts, ideas and facts in the dissertation. All the while, we were passionately physically restrained.

Secrecy about everything but the thesis was our mode. We agreed to this, unable and too frightened to speak to anyone about what was happening to us. Except that, as we sat talking in the car one night, conveniently parked in front of my apartment on Madison Avenue, he took my hand ever so gently, saying, "You know what's happening to us, don't you?"

What was happening to us? What was going on? This man was forbidden for women! This woman had another life!

Conversation ended as we folded into each other's arms in that little car. I was so relieved that he had taken the first step towards the truth of our love. I so feared being looked upon as a harlot, by him or by anyone else. It was too trite an explanation for our overflowing emotions.

I carried on with my professional life as if nothing had changed and feeling like a dirty liar. At first I told no one at the magazine, except my beloved assistant Dorothy, about the unorthodox relationship I was in. In the beginning, I didn't even tell Dorothy the truth. I just had to tell her why that priest would be calling the office. But she was too intuitive and intelligent to not figure out what was going on, especially since Father was calling at least once a week.

Bounding up the two flights of stairs, Father would arrive at my door, a yellow rose in hand. Manuel giggled one day, asking me, "How is the Roses Man?" He rolled the "r" dramatically with his Spanish accent. I should have known he would be alert to who was coming and going to my apartment!

We gave each other a lot of tests as the weeks went along. I, being more immature and more cynical, tested him more. I told him stories of my social life, emphasizing seductive scenes (real or almost real), bragging about the material status of men I dated, painting a picture of unremitting gaiety, romance and adventure. Never admitting his jealousy or fear about my life, he would humor me, undergo the test and lead me to the next level of trust.

Gradually I learned that he had a real and serious reason to finish his dissertation. "I need to get my degree so that I can leave the priesthood for a while and think about things. "I'm working on a plan. Don't worry. I'll take every single step they want me to take," he told me as we came closer to the end of our work. "Leave the priesthood!" I exclaimed. "Why? No, don't tell me. I know. But when, and how?"

This had been his plan all along, now revealed to me. It deepened the urgency of our work. I was thrilled. All those talks about faith and Catholicism now made more sense to me. He was questioning his faith and his priesthood before we met. The Second Vatican Council was the pivotal event that energized his decision to take a leave of absence.

The Council had opened in Rome in 1962, convened by Pope John XXIII, closing three years later on December 8, 1965. It followed, ninety-two years later, on the heels of the First Vatican Council, adjourned in 1870. It was that first Council which created the solemn definition of papal infallibility. Five popes came and went before the Second Vatican Council was proclaimed by Pope John. This beloved leader had a deep desire for *Aggiornamento*. When asked to reveal his intentions for the meeting he would, in the great Italian mode of using gesture, move to a window, throwing it open to let in a draught of fresh air.

He proclaimed he wanted "to increase the fervor and energy of Catholics, to serve the needs of Christian people." He wanted the church to be brought up to date, able to adapt to the challenging conditions of modern times. Ten commissions were established to study scripture, tradition, faith and morals, liturgy, seminaries and ecclesiastical studies, and more. At the opening, the pope addressed the two thousand five hundred priests gathered and told them that they had to find a way for the church to present itself to the world of the day and reach the minds and hearts of its faithful. What a brilliant insight! How exciting for those of us who had lost faith!

But, after years of struggle, the changes that were made in the church that most polarized people were changes in the liturgy. No more Mass in Latin. Priests must use the vernacular, face the people and discard "secret" prayers that only the priest could recite. No more fasting from midnight until next day's Communion (no wonder I fainted in church on a regular basis). Lots of other sacramental changes. No more fish on Friday. Music could be modern and inclusive. Non-Christians were no longer to be blamed for their ignorance of Christ and his church (the Catholic Church). Other churches were welcome to be in full communion with the Holy See.

Even in the midst of new openness from Vatican II, there was no discussion of the most crucial issues of a personal life, and no discussion of love, sex or marriage for the priesthood. The Roman Catholic tradition of celibacy was to be upheld. Women no longer had to wear hats in church, but their heads were still bowed. They could not be considered for the priesthood, could not administer sacraments. They could still wash the linens, assist the priest, teach the children and comfort the sick and dying.

We spent many a night obsessing on the lack of openness in the "new" church, frustrated with the church's inability to move away from its flawed traditions. We both wanted the institution to do what institutions struggle so to do. We wanted the church to risk opening its window with wisdom and courage and change because it exists to serve human need. That was not to be, we agreed. We grew up in a hard religion. And the miracle was that we agreed on all of this.

Father's rules for us in the apartment did work for a while. I stayed happily on my side of the "bundling board," teasing him every once in a while, "I need to come over to your side to check that footnote." But the rules were not to last, just as the new "open" church was not to be. I don't know when the boundaries ended. They just did. It was organic. We opened the windows in the spring and summer to let in the city air. We opened our hearts, bit by bit, testing, testing and testing. When would it crash, this trust? Who would retreat first? Who would close the window first? How far could we push it open?

Sacrumque Profanus

Father had no trouble justifying the enormous value of his daily work, laboring in the halls of high schools in Brooklyn, Queens and Long Island. The system took care of approximately one hundred fifty thousand youth in the heyday of the Catholic Church. He built big new school buildings for the increasing numbers of Catholic high school students of Brooklyn, Queens and Long Island, negotiated contracts for teachers and administrators, delivered endless graduation speeches, visited classrooms (always arriving cheerfully, his cassock robes swinging as he bounced around the room, telling a few jokes, disrupting the classroom and then leaving, to the annoyance of the teacher left in his wake). He loved his work, knew it had merit and was passionate about educational theory and practice. He was excited by new technology and its uses in the classroom and was also realistic about the practical circumstances he faced as nuns began leaving convents, creating the beginning of a staffing crisis for Catholic schools that only deepened as the century wore on.

Meanwhile, our own world settled into a weekly routine when we met Wednesdays at my apartment, first recounting to each other tales of our daily work, then on to a meal and to work on the thesis. I began to get glimpses of his real feelings as he intensely told me of some of his reflections on the future of the church. During our third dinner, he told me he was worried about the constant philosophical disputes he was having with some of his colleagues, not only just about educational theory, but, more importantly for him – and me – about the direction that the church was taking.

While performing the significant task of running the high a school system, he was dogged by the thesis deadline. During our fifth or sixth dinner he told me he had often been distracted by emergencies in his family. His manic-depressive sister would run away, and he would be called upon to join his father in finding her. His alcoholic brother would start drinking and then plunge into AA or into financial crisis and Father would be called upon to counsel him spiritually and materially. He was also "Unc,"a touchstone of stability for the eight nieces and nephews he adored. And he baptized all the family children, married the cousins and buried grandparents. His mother needed constant attention due to her persistent anxiety. There was no such thing as a boring day in her life. Everything was cause for high drama, illness or self-pity, and her son the priest was her designated fixer-upper. Only Pop, Father's father, needed nothing but basic filial love.

"You shouldn't want to have anything to do with me," he said one night. "My family is too much of a mess, too crazy." I was dying to meet them.

And what was he thinking in 1967 about the church he had joined years before when he was nineteen "because he loved Jesus," a church that at that time seemed to be accepting an increasing role for the laity and certainly the dissolution of absolutism? How unnerving it was for this mature man in his mid-thirties to have so many comfortable absolutes stripped away. One week in a confessional he would have to chastise a penitent for eating meat on Friday or not fasting before Sunday Communion. After the Second Vatican Council, that chastisement was obsolete, along with a woman's need to wear a hat in church and kneeling to receive Communion at the altar rail. What did not change, as promised in the early days of Vatican II, was the fiction that being a modern Catholic would mean more individual responsibility for one's actions, more discussion and debate about matters of faith and morals, more openness to all those who had been treated like lesser cogs in the corporation.

How silly my work seemed by contrast. *Harper's Bazaar* was all about fashion trends, color names, shoe tips and heels, important models of the moment, the peccadilloes of artists, photographers and other creative types in the world of Madison Avenue in the heyday of high fashion just prior to the heyday of sex, drugs and alcohol. I created a ridiculous argument about the relationship between a fashion magazine and the philosophical tenets of aesthetics. Luckily, I had taken a philosophy course in aesthetics in college, which I loved, and was able to call up some intellectual gobbledygook from time to time. I never got away with it, but Father was intrigued and unnerved by the world of my work. High style, big money, fast living, wretched excess, the pursuit of power and flash – these were all characteristics he attributed to my professional world. And they frightened him.

It became increasingly difficult to glamorize my world as Father and I worked closer and closer. When we were in my apartment, I gradually dropped the veil of glamour and success. "Your world is more stable than mine," I cried, "and you're hinting to me that you're planning to leave it. Where on earth are we going?"

I was pushing myself physically, working ten-hour days at the magazine, maintaining my social life and editing Father's work. Sleepless nights became nights of torture as exhaustion, fear and insecurity became my nocturnal companions. All my old Catholic demons visited my bed as I became more and more involved with this priest. My work must have suffered. It began to feel more frivolous and irrelevant. Critically, I would complain to my friends at work, "That editor has no idea what she's doing" or "I can't take the bitchiness much longer." I started making a habit of being late for work since I rarely went to sleep before 2 in the morning and often missed the morning alarm. No one seemed to notice, but I had to make enormous efforts to focus on the next photo shoot and the next promotion. I didn't dare risk losing my job.

The author, Mary Sheehan, at a tender age trying to figure out the world

The author's First Communion Day,
celebrating with siblings

The author's, Mary Sheehan, Harper's Bazaar official publicity photo

*Brokaw House, Fifth Avenue and 79th Street, New York (between ca. 1910
and ca. 1915) Future home of publishing offices of the Institute of
Electrical and Electronic Engineers (IEEE)
Library of Congress*

The camera catches Mary Sheehan of Harper's Bazaar, left, and pert New York mannequin Gail MacDermott between planes at International Airport. Gail is wearing Jerry Silverman's white and black silk-cotton tweed costume, one of a collection being shown in the air junket.

When Fashion Goes Sky-High

By AGNES McCAY
Fashion Editor

SKY-HIGH FASHIONS that look equally well on the ground, or anywhere for that matter, flew into International Airport this week on a cross-country junket under the auspices of four famous names.

The four sponsors were Jerry Silverman, Douglas Aircraft, Delta Airlines and Harper's Bazaar. The inspiration for this fashion-journey was the new Douglas DC-9 jet that will inaugurate short and medium hop service early in 1966.

Pictures of this sleek jet-beauty and the fashions modeled in flight by three New York mannequins are featured in six pages of the February issue of Harper's Bazaar.

Accompanying the three mannequins were Mary Sheehan of Harper's Bazaar, and Jerry Uchin of Jerry Silverman.

On the windswept airport for a brief half-hour before taking off for San Francisco, models Flo Smith, Debbie Franz and Gail MacDermott posed for pictures in Jerry Silverman costumes.

Their complete airborne wardrobe will make its down-to-earth debut tomorrow at the new Joseph Magnin store in Topanga Plaza (Canoga Park).

New York mannequin Flo Smith, right, poses at International Airport in Jerry Silverman's black and white silk and cotton

Some of the national publicity about the Douglas Delta promotion Fashions in Flight week
(Los Angeles Herald-Examiner; January 31, 1965)

Reverend William G. Scanlan's official ordination photograph, 1954

Brooklyn Diocesan Schools Leadership: Monsignor Henry M. Hald, Superintendent, Reverend Eugene J. Molloy, Associate Superindendent and Reverend William G. Scanlan, Assistant Superindendent (1960s)

One of the perks of being Assistant Superintendent, Father Scanlan representing the Brooklyn Diocesan Schools at the 1963 Queens Beauty Institute graduation

Routel Studio

FUTURE SCIENTISTS: Nine seniors at Bishop Loughlin Diocesan High School, Brooklyn, have won State Regents science scholarships. Pictured from the left: front row, Gerard Geary, Brother Basil Stephen, F.S.C., principal, Rev. William G. Scanlan, assistant diocesan superintendent of schools, and Patrick Cullinan; rear, Eugene Gaydos, James Oberst, John Szeligowski, Frank Russo, Charles Poole and Gary Jacobi. Dennis Cullinan was not present when picture was taken. Loughlin is is staffed by the Christian Brothers.

Father Scanlan honoring high school science scholars (1960s)

Jay Sharp

AT BISHOP'S EXERCISES opening the school year in the Diocese, held last Sunday at St. James-Pro Cathedral, were some 6,000 members of educational staffs in the diocesan school system, both Religious and lay. Above, with His Excellency, who presided, are Mother M. Celeste, O.P., diocesan supervisor in the Brooklyn Diocese for the Amityville Sisters of St. Dominic and chairman of the elementary science curriculum committee, and Brother Medard, C.F.X, new principal of Xaverian High School, Bay Ridge. Standing are, from left: Rev. Eugene J. Molloy, associate superintendent, and Rt. Rev. Msgr. Henry M. Hald, diocesan superintendent of schools; Very Rev. William Granger Ryan, president of Seton Hill College, Greensburg, Pa., a Brooklyn priest, who gave the principal address at the exercises, and Rev. William G. Scanlan, assistant superintendent of diocesan schools.

Opening of school year with His Excellency Bryan J. McEntegart (1960s)

The Great Alleluia Day, January 17, 1968

Will and Mary celebrating in 1994

*Will at a **Sing for Hope** piano at Lincoln Center, New York, with the author in the background. The piano was painted by Matisse's granddaughter (2010-photo courtesy of Sing for Hope)*

IN NOMINE PATRIS

At the beginning of the traditional Catholic Mass in Latin, the priest stands at the first step of the altar, chanting *"In Nomine Patris"* – "In the Name of the Father." It's a solemn beginning to prayer, invoking the Trinity – the Father, Son and Holy Spirit – to anoint the ceremony, in this case the introductory prayers of the Mass. It's a phrase that always signaled, for me, the start of something important.

The Name of the Father was a big issue as we began our special Wednesday night restaurant ritual. What was once a serious and intense work night became an equally serious and intense non-work night. It was now a night to enjoy each other, to deal with the days and to figure out our future, together or independently.

Father's thesis was submitted on time, and we were now, in the springtime of 1967, discovering love and fun, danger and excitement. Each week, one of us would find the place and make a reservation for dinner, in my name. I stayed dressed in the design of the day. Father did his Superman routine, changing from his professional clothes to ordinary male attire. The tie was a serious issue. Most restaurants in those days required a tie. Father owned only one. The fashion editor became the purchaser of a few ties and shirts that were then closeted in my apartment. Such a mundane issue was a huge symbol of change and liberation.

We never went back to the same restaurant, instead exploring out-of-the way places in Manhattan and Brooklyn, always checking when we walked in the door for a parishioner, a fellow priest, a Madison Avenue colleague, a relative. Approaching the site was a moment of high tension, and we never fully relaxed while we were dining. Our other social activity was movies. Again, Father donned his secular duds, uncomfortable and self-conscious at first, and off we would go into the world, practicing being a couple. We carefully scanned the line in front of the theater, and if we saw anyone we knew, we walked away. We only saw people we knew a couple of times, but it was always a shattering experience.

We had so much to talk about. For starters, there was the status of the church as it tossed about in the waters of change, unable to change, trying to change and changing so many non-fundamental things. Guitars were replacing the organ in church. It seemed that everybody had to kiss or hug everybody for the sign of peace. Kneeling for an hour became a thing of the past. Nuns could get out of their habits. Discipline and liturgical details were updated to the 20th century, but much doctrine remained smack in the Middle Ages. Priestly celibacy was reaffirmed. Divorce was still unacceptable. Birth control and abortion continued to be forbidden.

Father worried about the possibility that he could no longer live and work as a priest. And that was the moment I accidentally came into his life. (Some would say there are no accidents in life.) The man I met was a man who showed a great capacity to love, a thoughtful and respectful man with an ever-curious mind. Ironically, it was the assurances that doctrine promised, the absoluteness of everything, which had encouraged to him as a young man to choose priesthood. Now the foundation of his faith was eroding, and he questioned everything.

"I could always be sure about morals, discipline, liturgy, doctrine," he said one night during dinner at a cozy Italian restaurant on the Lower East Side. "But one day, it was a mortal sin to eat meat on

Friday, and the next day it wasn't! What happened to the people who ate meat on Friday before the change happened and died? Did they go to hell? And that's only a minor change!"

While these questions were torturing Father, they bothered me as well, but not to the same degree. After all, it was his vocation, his life at risk. For me, the changes and the lack of changes in the church were yet another excuse for my anger at the institution.

One night at dinner in a little restaurant somewhere near the Brooklyn Bridge (which his grandfather, an ironworker, helped to build) I began an awkward conversation.

"Umm, I feel a little funny calling you Father or calling you nothing," I said. "What would you like me to call you?"

"Well," he said, "My mother calls me Billy, my Father does too, but he also calls me William. My friends call me Willy. My really old friends call me Skippy. Some people call me Bill."

Twirling my pasta around on my fork, I thought about those names and said them aloud. None felt right.

"May I call you Will?" I asked shyly, gulping down a mouthful of pasta. "My grandfather was Will. My adored grandfather, I might add." Father was charmed. From thence, Will was the name of the Father.

And so we, Will and Mary, began our journey from Herbert Street in Brooklyn to Madison Avenue in New York, from the rectory to my apartment, to a life together. Like the children of Israel, we were "straitened in the land," shut in by the desert. Our desert, however, was not ancient arid land but a vibrant city with certain spoken and unspoken social mores for Catholics and others alike. And, like the children of Israel, we needed a parting of the waters to reach our promised land. We had no idea where we were going. We had only a vague idea of where we were.

PARTING OF THE WATERS

It was close to midnight. The crew was packing up after a day-long photo shoot at the new home of the Metropolitan Opera at Lincoln Center. We had been doing the photography for a multi-page spread in the magazine in this exciting new hot spot in New York. The shoot featured sumptuous evening gowns under the magnificent Austrian chandeliers that lowered and rose at key moments in the opera house and lit everything underneath them with a beatific glow.

Who could not feel glorious, blessed and holy in this place? It was considered a successful day since we completed all the photos, the models had been very professional, the photographer was not a prima donna, the editor was calm and the fashion was impeccable. I was thrilled with the results, exhilarated by the rituals. Get the coffee, schmooze with the models so that they're in a good mood, bow to the photographer so that he's in a good mood, give the evil eye to the assistants so that they keep things moving, arrange the set up so that makeup and hair can be done easily, press and hang the garments in the order of the shoot, keep the hairdresser on the set from fumigating all of us with hair spray, thank the opera house staff over and over again as we needed to get to sensitive areas in the building, keep the curious crowds away from each setting, get the coffee, get the lunch, find the telephones to make an emergency call, keep track of the time for the booking agency. Ah, the glamour of it all!

I had spent the day monitoring the creases, pulling and pushing clothing on and off some young woman's lovely body, changing earrings, bracelets, necklaces and shoes excessively until they were perfect. Behind that flowing skirt could be a dozen pins crimping one fold perfectly in place. At the back of the bodice could be Scotch tape holding one sleeve precisely on the shoulder, clamps between shoulder blades pulling the top every so seductively across the breast. Paper clips would do in a pinch to keep a belt in place, keep a pleat in just the right spot on a hip. The shoes could be stuffed with whatever product was around so that they fit. Jewelry would be affixed with Scotch tape too if a clasp wasn't working right. And through it all, the model had to hold a pose that a yogi would be hard-pressed to sustain.

At the end of a day like this I had a great feeling of accomplishment and delight in the quality of the work we had all achieved. I bade farewell to the few colleagues left at the photo site. Most had already left, and it was my responsibility to clean up our mess. My work would continue after the photo shoot, creating the promotional materials the magazine would distribute across the country to fashion buyers and merchandise managers in high-end shops. The photo spread that appeared in print three months later was a successful commercial piece for all involved. We might do a press campaign or a catalogue. We might go out to those stores as guest editors to meet the press and serve as commentators for a fashion show.

And at the end of that long day, the best part of my day began. Will was waiting for me at the fountain at Lincoln Center, anxious to hear about my adventures, happy to walk me home from work. I was so happy to see him, so exhilarated by the secrecy we were still maintaining.

"Hi, Father," I greeted him. I still called him that in public. "How was your day?" I asked, eager to be part of his important work. He started his list, "Well, I started my day with prayer, spent the morning at the office trying to understand the importance of television to the school system, slipped out for a game of squash at noon, came back to meetings, had dinner at the rectory, and here I am. With you."

We left Lincoln Center. Rounding the corner of Madison Avenue and 60th Street, I was busy gabbing about the day, still caught up in the excitement of it and hadn't noticed Will's sudden and unusual quietness.

"I know you love your work, but I worry about the hours you keep. They're crazy, and yet you love it," he said. "Life with me may not be that glamorous. What if we decide to stay together and move from New York? We may have to leave New York. It's going to be too scandalous, our coming together. The bishop might do something. I don't know if I can get a job here like the one I have. It might be hard to find another place where I can run a school system the size of the Brooklyn Diocese. The bishop might see that I'm blackballed. I don't know if I can get a job. I don't know if I can live like a normal human being in the world. I know you really love your work."

The paper clips and Scotch tape and staples behind the scene jumped out at me. The glamour of the day dissipated.

"That's the reality. It looks perfect, but it really isn't," I thought. "And yet I love it. Do I want that for the rest of my life? Or do I want the flesh and blood and imperfection and everyday humdrum of life?"

To say it was easy to walk away from success and power and elegance is not the truth. To say that real life would be imperfection and humdrum is also not true. My young heart was aching with desire for both, and I was lost.

LOVE

Reality

COMMUNION

Intimacy happened long before sex and had nothing and everything to do with sex. I keep thinking we had known each other for years. But it was actually less than a year before we were deeply, wondrously in love. None of that was planned. Producing a dissertation was planned. Love and commitment were not anywhere in the original agreement.

In the Catholic ritual of Communion today, the priest faces the congregation after blessing the bread and wine, symbolic of the body and blood of Jesus, and says, "Take this, all of you and eat this, for this is my body. Take this all of you and drink from it, for this is my blood." Since my college days, my spiritual response to the intent of this ritual had been negative and, if the truth be told, irreverently derisive.

The symbolism of the Mass as a meal, the sacred sharing of a meal, had long lost its meaning for me, and I thought it needed to be updated. Sadly, I also thought it had long lost its meaning to the faithful as well, just as our national holidays have been transformed from their original source of meaning and become food and drink party days. I felt that the modernization trappings that the church had applied to the Mass after Vatican II were merely cosmetic. And I knew about cosmetic! It was convenient to have Mass in English, it was encouraging to have girls serving on the altar, it was hopeful that there was an inclusive congregation-wide kiss of peace. But the old symbol remained, forgotten or never known by many, too complicated for most except those living mystical monastic lives.

Our commitment was intensifying, becoming like the personal meditation after Communion. Not part of the actual liturgy of the Mass, this was a time while the other members of the congregation were receiving Communion to reflect on the intimate and wonderful union between you and Christ that had just occurred in Communion I usually came to a place of peace at this part in the service.

"Mass is an outdated symbol," Father said one evening. I breathed a sigh of relief when he made that statement one night while we were working. I wouldn't have dared to say that, fearing that I would offend him. I knew from the start that he wasn't like my parish priest of old, but, in the early days of working with him, I couldn't pinpoint the difference.

We constantly marveled at it, because of our different ages, our different families, our different education, our different professions. That bond was wondrous and the basis for deep and lasting intimacy that was so strong that it guided us through the perils and storms that were to come. And it guided us to that moment that we agreed that becoming lovers was the next, inevitable step in our relationship. The conversation leading to that decision was grim and deep.

"Am I doing you an injustice in agreeing with any circumstances other than across a desk or a table? By insisting on those circumstances only, will we prove something? Or is that forcing unnatural, artificial boundaries, which may not be right?" I wrote him in a tortured note.

Celibacy was a promise that Father had taken seriously. Will had not been involved with a woman since he entered the seminary and said goodbye to the love of his young manhood. He knew my social history only too well until we decided it was not a good idea for me to keep answering his questions about my dates. So we were coming together with different sexual histories but not with a different mindset about sexuality.

The conversation eludes me today, but the memory of the import of our decision will never leave me. It was the next, organic step for us. One night, after an intense but short work session, we talked about what was happening between us. We carefully sat in our assigned spots on either side of the bundling board as the sexual tension mounted. And then there was that beautiful moment when Will rose from the couch and came to my chair, tenderly, oh so tenderly, tracing the outline of my face with his gentle hands and guiding me from the chair. To love. All other facets of that wondrous time between us remain between us. The bond was sealed.

Communion, the consumption of another's body and blood in respect and love, is what comes to my mind when I think of our intimacy. There were certainly awkward moments, awkward conversations to come. But the symbolism of uniting us was life-changing. I should have felt guilty. In the world's eyes, I was seducing a priest. I never thought of our relationship that way. Many years later I began to realize that people who were upset with us in 1967 were people who thought that I had acted like a brazen red-headed Jezebel. I always assumed folks were upset because, in their eyes, he had abandoned his priesthood.

We were both given strong training in guilt – the Irish-American brand. Yet when it came to our loving intimacy, neither of us ever felt guilt. We were certainly overwhelmed with love, with confusion, with the ease of our coming together. It was so thrilling that we wanted to tell everyone. But ours could not be a public tale yet. It was a secret ritual, although not a wicked or salacious one. Like the Communion ceremony we had grown up with, it was a deeply private and intimate relationship.

POST COMMUNION

Post Communion for Will and me was anything but quiet and reflective. I was dying to tell my cousin who had introduced us and to confess to her, my younger sister and my two dearest friends to know about this miracle in my life. Dorothy, my assistant, was getting very suspicious of Father Scanlan's daily phone calls. I so wanted to share my joy. But the dissertation had to be submitted, and the bishop had to be told that Father "could no longer represent this organization." Will and I were putting together a strategic plan for his future, we thought, but the stress of our secret was more than we could bear. The public cost of disclosing our secret was enormous. The personal cost of not disclosing our secret was overwhelming. It was too hard to keep the secret.

We needed to try to have some kind of social life outside of our work. How could we move from our intimate world to the public world? We felt an enormous pressure to tell our story to someone else, just to get a reaction. We were expecting, "What are you? Nuts? Stop this right away before he gets caught!" We needed a reality check. We needed a sanity check.

Will thought of the perfect pair.

Gene and Jackie Fontinell were part of a Catholic liberal reform loyal opposition group. Will knew them through his band of priest and laity friends who were studying Vatican II and the issues and potential movements of the moment. Gene was a professor in the philosophy department at Queens College when I was a student, an accomplished philosopher, popular with his colleagues, beloved by the students. To their sorrow they were childless, which gave them endless excuses to adopt all kinds of causes and people in their lives.

Will called and asked if he could see them and bring along a friend, a woman who was editing his dissertation. They must have sensed something in his voice and invited us for dinner at their home. Although I was more scared than usual when meeting someone new, Will assured me they would be kind no matter what they thought of our situation. Indeed they were kind and greeted me warmly at the front door. During our pre-dinner drinks, I began to relax as the Fontinells talked with us as if we were like any other couple, not four-headed monsters. At dinner, we discussed our common beliefs that the church was in need of radical change. And we told them our secret. I'm sure they weren't one bit surprised when Will said, "Well, you must know that Mary and I have fallen in love." They reacted with calm and were attentive to our every word as we told them our story.

"Keep going. We're with you. We'll help you." They blessed us. As we hit the cold air, I started crying and couldn't stop for the next hour.

Their kindness and support were more than I ever expected. Will joined me in tears as we gathered the courage to continue on our path. We still weren't sure where the path was leading, but we knew we wanted to stay the course.

Somehow I went on with my professional life at the magazine, loving the work, the success and the challenges. I also continued my personal life, seeing my friends, even continuing dating the two men I had been going out with for a while. But it was all a charade. I soon told those two men that I was seriously involved with another man, without revealing who he was or what he did. We agreed, in both cases, to remain friends. In fact, both remained friends for many, many years. Both were invited to our wedding. One of them came.

One of them would also play a pivotal role in helping Will and me make a decision to go forward with a life together. He was a successful Hollywood producer, sophisticated man of the world, former husband of a couple of well-known American actresses. He was a generous and loving person, a lover in every sense of the word. One of his loves was problem solving. One morning I awoke with an unidentified rash all over my body. When I was describing it and the details of my wonderful relationship to him, he immediately suggested a California vacation at his expense. A struggling Catholic, he was amused at first by my confession of love for Will. "It would make a great movie," he joked. As he became more involved in my situation, however, he became sympathetic, angry at the church for what he saw as outdated beliefs and policies.

He was a close friend of my publisher but sworn to secrecy about my situation. My publisher adored him, was awed by him and would follow any suggestions that the producer made. I had plenty of vacation time available, so I knew I could request and receive a two-week vacation. I did and away I went with my rash for a February Beverly Hills adventure.

I knew, however, that Dorothy had to be brought into our circle. Having worked with her for more than a year in challenging circumstances and with trade secrets at our disposal, I knew I could trust her. I also knew she had been through her own messy situation with her husband since she was his second wife and worked with him prior to their marriage. So I told Dorothy the truth about my relationship with Will. In her ever-efficient, ever-trusting and calming voice, she agreed also to be my assistant of secrets. She was most discrete. From then on she always came into my office to quietly announce Father was on the phone, and never asked questions. I headed to California, knowing that my professional life would be safeguarded from my personal life.

Will secretly whisked me to the airport. For the first time we spoke the words that maybe, perhaps, we couldn't go on. Maybe the rash meant something deeply malevolent. He suggested that upon my return, we would finish our work together in a month. Then he would take the next step in his life, and I would continue with mine at the magazine. He would spend a year or so to see if he could function in a life outside the priesthood. We could keep in touch from a distance, he said.

I cried most of the way to Los Angeles. I was staying with mutual friends of the producer and mine, also film people, in their beautiful home in the Sherman Oaks section of Beverly Hills. They knew I was having a relationship problem, but not the specifics. In order to cheer me up, they arranged one party after another with Hollywood stars who were their friends. I was miserable all the while until Valentine's Day 1967 when I received a telegram from Will, "All bets are off. I'll pick you up at the airport when you return."

My host and hostess thought that their wonderful parties had helped change my mood. It wasn't until the end of the year that I could tell them the truth and thank them for putting up with me for those long two weeks. I blissfully returned to New York, the rash healed, ready to walk through the next steps with Will, positive, confident, full of hope.

FOOD

A few weeks later I was hungrily searching for a setting to present Will to more friends. I whipped up an idea. Now that we had been nourished and strengthened by the support of the Fontinells, now that the rash was gone, I was ready for a grand introduction of the man to people who mattered to me.

Meanwhile, the thesis was not only submitted but also immediately accepted.

With great care, I invited thirty friends for dinner, telling them that I wanted them to meet the man whom I had been working with, to celebrate the completion of his thesis. Of course, it was a transparent invitation to everyone but me. My friends had now been offered little tidbits of information about Will and me, but not the full menu. I had no idea I was so obvious about my feelings toward the man.

It felt as if the entire early summer was devoted to planning and preparing the presentation of this event. It took over my life as if it were a state occasion. Once I had the guest list and invitation settled, I wrestled with the menu for a meal for thirty in my little flat. It would be challenge to prepare it in the kitchen formerly known as a mop closet, to find the plates and knives, forks and spoons, glassware and napkins and chairs for all those people. No paper, of course. Never considering budget or a caterer, I forged ahead. I wanted to put on a culinary show for Will and my friends.

Curried veal paprika for thirty. Aha! That was the solution. Veal was dramatic. It would make a statement about me as a sophisticated gourmand. Just add poppy-seed noodles and a green salad, I decided, and some good bread. No, I wouldn't make the bread this time. Wine and water would be fitting drinks. And then coffee and some desserts purchased from Greenberg's, the nearby pastry palace.

For the next few weeks my spare minutes were spent mounting the event. I rented a garment rack to place in the hallway outside my flat. This arrangement gave me a chance to talk with my neighbor for the first time in months. Even though we were the only tenants on the floor, we hardly saw each other, peacefully co-existing in easy-going, non-intimate city life. He agreed to the garment rack and graciously declined my invitation to the party.

I arranged to rent a buffet table, linens, flatware, dishes and glasses and then turned to the kitchen. My *Harper's Bazaar* colleague and dear friend Faith, living a block away, whom I had introduced to Will, whom I confided in once our secret was slightly public, offered her real-kitchen equipment and space as a backup to my faux kitchen. I would prepare the veal in advance and store some of it in Faith's refrigerator. Even though I had a full-size fridge, there would never be enough room for the size of this dish.

I chopped and seared and stirred batches of the main dish at home, multiplying "serves eight" by four, schlepping each batch up Madison Avenue as it was completed. Faith's role was to return the batches to my place the next day, where I would put it all together to reheat in the mop closet. It was an all-day, all-night preparation, so I took a vacation day from the magazine, happy to be playing with this domestic distraction.

The minute I got out of bed the morning of the party, I moved as much furniture as possible into my bedroom, and pushed the remaining pieces close to the walls. The rentals arrived without a hitch and were delivered up the marble staircase. I set up the buffet table along the mirrored wall. After covering it with the creamy linen rental cloth, I arranged the flowers from my favorite shop on Lexington Avenue into a tall, lush bouquet that reflected beautifully from the mirror. White candles, wine glasses and breadbaskets adorned the table set with the rented plates, forks, knives and spoons. I tossed the salad, kept the homemade dressing aside until serving time, set the noodles up for later preparation and placed cheese and crackers around the room in strategic places. I tried to remain calm.

A long hot shower helped my nerves. While I was dressing I ran through the list of guests and tried not to guess how they would react to Will, reminding myself of the purpose of this event. Was I doing this to impress people, to have people approve of my relationship, to get support, to spread my joy? It was hard for me to admit that I was hoping to achieve all of those things.

When Will arrived before the guests, my heart was fluttering away, but my head was comforted and convinced. I knew, for sure, this was the right person for me even though all the circumstances were wrong. We danced around the few feet of clear space in the living room, joyfully anticipating sharing our story, until it was time to put the culinary details in motion. He was a willing, if inexperienced, sous chef, obviously delighted with the preparations as he pitched in following my rapid-fire instructions.

The flat was bathed in candlelight, and the aromas were soon flowing down the stairs to the front door. Back to back, shoulder to shoulder, toe to toe, friends bumped into each other as they dove into the food and wine, hardly able to lift a fork to mouth in the available space. It was a warm and delicious night, the best love feast on Madison Avenue, full of ayes and absent nays.

VESTING, DIVESTING

When we moved to our first home, I requested that my husband dispose of the last remnant of his vestments, his Roman collar, which symbolically bound a man to his priestly vocation. We joked about tossing it out along with the "Clergy" sign that got us parking anywhere in the world. Underneath the joking was a deep desire on my part to get rid of what I thought was a creepy neck accessory.

Our relationship was rapidly unfolding. Chapter by chapter, piece by piece, his plan revealed itself to him and to me. All through that spring, as final touches were made to the thesis, we would discuss his future, our future. He couldn't stay in the church any longer. He would have the credentials to get a job "outside" once he was awarded his degree. He would figure out how to tell his bishop. He would see continue to see his psychiatrist. He would go on a retreat and talk to his confessor.

"I can no longer represent this organization," he would say, his body sagging with the weight of this revelation. "All my life. All I every wanted to be was a priest. I must be crazy. I have to know if I am."

There was the joyous day when the thesis was submitted to the doctoral committee at NYU. We had decided upon a strategy for success, submitting the document completely finished rather than submitting three chapters at a time. We took the risk that when the committee saw the whole, done, formatted, typed, charts and graphs drawn, they would have a hard time picking it apart again and would pass on it. We were right. It sailed through the committee, no revisions, nothing but glowing comments. This victory must have given us the courage to proceed. By spring we were discussing the future, looming large for Father, as his graduation day was approaching.

He attended his commencement, accompanied and cheered on by his mother and father. In the midst of all of this he was given the university's highest academic award and had to attend that ceremony as well. "This doesn't mean a thing to me right now," he said when told he had to attend another ceremony to accept the award. He was now consumed with when, what and how to speak to his bishop. That event in itself demanded a whole plan.

How I understood all that he was revealing! I, who used to go to daily Mass, praying constantly for guidance to the Virgin Mary, promising good behavior in exchange for forgiveness. I, who proudly lead my class into the church for benediction, special holy day masses and assemblies. I, who was stalked by a couple of nuns because they thought I was a perfect candidate for their religious order, had achieved a level of disdain, disbelief and rage at the church before I was in my twenties. My distress with the church drove me away from the doors I so loved to open early in the morning, from the perfume of incense, from the glory of the organ's sound, from the solemnity and pomp of high mass, from the sureness and sameness, from the belief that this institution was telling the truth, the only truth, the one, holy and apostolic truth.

We continued to be amazed that we had arrived at the same place from such different lands, on such different paths, at such different times in our lives. This marvel propelled us forward. We explored our relationship, laying out the garments week by week, airing our dirty linens, undressing ourselves bit by bit until we got to the naked truth about each other. Our relationship was no longer skin deep. We somehow knew we had to remove all protective clothing if we were going to take the next step.

THE LAST WEEKEND

Finally, it was the last weekend Father would ever professionally hear the confession of another human being. And we were the only people in the world who knew his agenda for the weekend. My adrenaline was pumping for days as we carefully planned the details of the weekend, with as much care and calculation as if it were a major special event.

Well, it was.

We met at my apartment Friday night after we had finished our work for the week – he at the Education Office, me at the magazine. I had hardly slept during the week. Will was calm and mature about the upcoming event. We had agreed to eat dinner at home so that we could organize our thoughts and actions for the next few days. He had some writing to do. I experimented with some gourmet cuisine, for my own amusement and distraction.

We carefully, with scriptures, dictionary and thesaurus in hand, crafted his Sunday sermon on that Friday night, knowing it would be his last priestly sermon. The Sunday Mass talk was supposed to be a commentary on the Gospel read at the Mass each week, reflecting a particular time in the liturgical year. A priest always knew what the topic of his sermon would be long before he mounted the steps to the pulpit, so that theoretically, he had plenty of time for preparation.

Knowing this was his finale, Will tried to be positive and hopeful in his message while referring to the Gospel of that particular Sunday.

He knew that the parishioners would be shocked by his departure and he wanted to leave them with a comforting message. His sensitivity to them on this occasion was particularly touching to me. Finally, this thoughtful preacher was confident that his sermon reflected his thinking, albeit metaphorical in part, that all things must change. He worked late into the night on his message, checking with me from time to time to get my reaction to a word or thought.

We spent Saturday together until early afternoon, doing the kind of tasks that couples do – shopping, laundry, straightening up. I never seemed to get on top of the mess in my apartment, probably because it was so small and I had too many clothes, too many shoes, too many books and too little time for organizing, hanging up and putting stuff away. Will was tolerant of this most of the time, unless he was spending more than a couple of hours in my clutter.

Around 3 p.m. on Saturday he left. I was nervous and giddy saying good-bye, knowing I would not see him alone again until Sunday morning. His destination was St. Gerard's Church in Queens. Ironically, this was the site of his baptism and early education. Ever since he left the life of a parish priest and became an administrator, he had been going to this church on weekends as a helper, hearing confessions on Saturday and saying Mass on Sunday. The parish was so large and active that the three priests who lived there needed assistance with their weekly tasks.

Father arrived at the church and went directly to the confessional box he always used, settling in for what on this day would be more of an endurance test than anything else. None of those confessing their wrongdoings to him knew that they would never encounter him in that role again. After the evening stint was finished, he drove to his parents' home nearby and slept there for what was to be his last weekend night functioning actively as a priest.

Our plan was that I would borrow my father's car on some pretext. Dad was in the hospital in Queens recovering from a heart ailment. Early Sunday morning, I picked up the car in Queens, promising to visit him at the hospital later in the day and drove to St. Gerard's. I arrived at the church and shyly entered, my face burning with embarrassment. I hoped to find a seat in the rear. I was convinced that every person in that church knew that I was Father's love. There was no seat available in the rear, but I found a pew in the front and slid in, hoping no one would notice me. In fact, no one in the church knew me or noticed me at all.

My heart raced with love as Father bounded onto the altar decked out in his Mass vestments. I had never seen him in this role. He was wonderfully himself – energetic, friendly, compassionate, funny and serious all at once, even while wearing all that medieval garb.

At the Gospel section of the Mass he approached the pulpit, turned on the microphone and started laughing. He then composed himself and read the Gospel for the day solemnly and then, looking out at the congregation, said, "Well, folks, I've carefully prepared a sermon for you today. But for all my care, it has nothing to do with today. It's a sermon for next week's Gospel, and who knows if any of us will be here next week? So, here's the sermon for next week." I was the only person in that congregation who knew of the significance of his words and the magnitude of his mistake.

Mass ended, I left the church, again trying to be as invisible as possible. I didn't connect with Father. As he conversed with the congregation outside the church doors, I drove to the hospital, as I had promised, to visit my father. He had no idea where I had just been. I was mightily uncomfortable with my deception. Back in the city, I unwittingly parked Dad's car in a no-parking zone on Madison Avenue.

It was hours before Father and I met again. We were able to laugh heartily and nervously about his gaff. Clearly, his last sermon, as well as the man, was ahead of its time in the church.

On Monday morning, I went to get the car and return it to my parents. It wasn't parked where I had left it. I called the police to say my car had been stolen, only to be told that it had been towed because it was illegally parked. Now late for work, with more deception clouding my head, I schlepped to the Hudson River piers where towed cars were impounded, paid a large fine and returned the car to my parents without ever discussing the details of the life-changing weekend.

ILLA FORMA
The Plan

Pale yellow light crept into the sky over Brooklyn and Manhattan. Will awoke and knelt by the bed in his large rumpled but comfortable bedroom in the rectory, reciting morning prayers. Later in the day, for as long as he was a priest and even after his final Mass, he would recite the daily prayers of his breviary, the Book of Hours. "Just keeping the rules," he would say when I asked him why he practiced this daily routine when he had such major doubts and was taking such life changing steps.

I awoke, dangled my legs over the edge of the twin bed in my tiny closet of a bedroom, and took a deep drag on my Pall Mall. It was late spring of 1967. A few minutes later the phone rang with the now daily "This is your heavenly wake-up call" voice whispering seductively into my ear. This was sometimes the only moment in the day when we had a chance to be utterly personal with each other.

We were spending every available minute together, few as they were, intense and wonderful minutes, serious and silly. I was gradually sloughing off my other relationships with other men and at the same time telling my dearest friends of my forbidden love for a priest. Friends were invariably happy for me, although worried about the difficulties of the path I was taking. Bit by bit I introduced them to my beloved as opportunity arose.

"Marian's coming to town tonight," I said, referring to a good friend I wanted him to meet. "Maybe you can come over tonight and meet her." Living in Washington, D.C., she was coming for a long overdue weekend with me. She and I grabbed dinner around the corner and came back to my apartment, got in our pajamas and settled in for talk. With trepidation, and testing out her reactions, I carefully and hesitantly described what as going on in my life. "Well, it turns out that I've met this guy, and umm, he happens to be a priest and, well, um, um, I think I'm in love with him." Never one to be indecisive, she responded, "Tell him I want to meet him tonight."

We were already in our pajamas, but she demanded that I phone Will on the spot and ask him to come and meet her. Will knew she was an important friend of mine, so he came over half an hour later, dressed in Bermuda shorts and polo shirt. Marian, who was Jewish, was so shocked at his attire that she blurted out, "I've never met a priest in Bermuda shorts before!" To which he responded, "I've never met a lawyer in pajamas!" They took an instant and lifelong liking to each other. I could feel my body crumpling with relief that Marian approved. One more hurrah for us.

Will had talked to a few priest friends who were sorrowful or offended but not surprised. They were either envious or challenged by his decision to ask for a leave of absence from the priesthood. None of them asked to meet me except his best friend Tony, a seminary classmate and colleague in the Education Office. Tony and I loved each other at first sight. Warm, willing to stand by the side of his friend, he had no plans to leave his ministry. "I know Willy needs to move on," he said to me. "For me, I'm really happy and content doin' what I'm doin'."

Now that the thesis was submitted we had a new challenge – who to talk to, who to tell, how to get a leave of absence. That was the next step. Not marriage, not commitment. Just a next step. We were a couple. Period. And I would be as much help to him as I could be, with no commitments, I thought.

As luck would have it, my work at *Bazaar* was increasingly interesting and demanding. My publisher had promised me a successful career that he planned to personally orchestrate. Wanting me to try different spots in the magazine to see which I preferred, he promised me the prized trip to Paris for the spring collections. Although his motives were unclear to me, I was having a professional ball. I was meeting fascinating people, learning a lot about writing, photography and layout and design, about business, about putting a magazine together, about myself. I was a golden girl at the magazine, and I knew it, although I denied it. My head was pounding with professional success. My heart was heaving with love. The dark days of condemnation were not yet upon me and Will.

Will decided that he would stay in the superintendent's office through the school year, for the sake of his colleagues. In the meantime, he would prepare his resume for a new position outside the church.

"It's about time that I do this," he said. "I've been thinking about is since 1965." My initial sense of his feelings about his priesthood was confirmed. And it was confirmed that his decision to change his life had begun before I came on the scene. He had come through his darkest days, it was time to write the bishop and ask for a leave of absence.

SCANDAL

Commitment

84 Herbert Street
Brooklyn, NY

August 1, 1967

Archbishop Bryan J. McEntegart
241 Clinton Avenue
Brooklyn, New York 11205

Dear Archibishop:

After much thought, prayer and consultation, I am requesting a one-year leave of absence from the school office and from the diocese, as of September 1, 1967.

I am making my request at this time when the school year is completed, our staff has one location, and the High School Department is organized and functioning.

I have been considering such a move for more than two years, and am not making my request in anger or unhappiness. My priestly and professional associates are of the highest caliber. I am not protesting, beginning a movement, or making a dramatic gesture. On the contrary, I want to clarify my thinking by adopting a different perspective.

My work as a diocesan official and a secular priest requires great dedication. Such dedication, in its turn, demands a clear vision of the required tasks and their inter-relationships. My vision has become unclear. The requisite dedication has changed direction, become less ready, less strong.

In my judgement, the diocesan school office, the diocese, and the entire Church needs unity, unanimity, and, perhaps, even uniformity. Because I have many questions about the assumptions, procedures, attitudes, and values of the organizations I serve, my service is not such that I deem compatible with and requisite for the needs of these organizations. This must be my judgement, since no one else has the data upon which I base my decision.

My four and a half years of pastoral experience, eight and a half years of professional experience, my advanced studies, and the value of these to the diocesan school office, the diocese and the Church, is diluted and off-set by my cloudy vision, changing dedication and increasing questionings. Therefore, I seriously and firmly judge that my request for a leave of absence is the most reasonable, honest and honorable course of action I can take.

I have sought the advice and counsel of my parents and good friends, both religious and lay. But, in the end, the decision is mine.

I shall be happy to follow any procedure you think best.

Sincerely,
(Rev.) William G. Scanlan

EXCEL, EXCELLENT, EXCELLENCE, YOUR EXCELLENCY

On that hot and humid Friday, August 4, 1967, Will went to the meeting with the His Excellency, the Archbishop. He had been summoned to the bishop's Brooklyn office within days after he had sent the letter requesting a leave of absence. This was the first step in his separation from a twenty-two-year commitment which had really started two years earlier, in 1965, when the world of the Catholic Church was reeling with change.

That Friday, I slipped into a magenta-red linen A-line sleeveless dress while he methodically – and for the last time in his life – put on his white collarless shirt with the French cuffs, fastened the black rabbet over it, snapped in his collar and finished his outfit with his black suit. I left the apartment and started my walk to the office with anxiety and fear rising up in my throat. I had made an excuse to leave the office at noon for the weekend. Will left my apartment at the same time, head high, jaw set, serious and determined, heading for his car parked on Madison Avenue, and then driving the Beetle across the Brooklyn Bridge to the office of the bishop.

Guessing that we might need relief from the enormity of the occasion, we had made plans to escape the city. As soon as the meeting with His Excellency was over, we would get into the already-packed car and head for the Berkshires to spend a weekend enjoying music at Tanglewood, breathing, relaxing, and getting some space from our reality. Although we didn't know it at the time, it was a brilliant plan that effectively kept each of us focused throughout that momentous day on something pleasant.

That whole summer was a strange time. Will spent occasional weekdays and weekends at my place, which had become the bunker, the nest and the conference center of our lives. I would throw myself into the day at *Harper's Bazaar*, accomplishing the work set out for me, riding on a cloud of success. I was still hiding my other life from most of my colleagues. My discomfort only deepened when one day my director told me that, in addition to being sent on the coveted trip to the Paris spring collections, I would have a windowed office when the magazine moved to its new headquarters on Fifth Avenue the following year. "You'd better not leave," she threatened, "'cause the plans are for you to be in a plum office." I'm sure I blushed knowing that I would probably never sit in that prized spot nor ever go to the Paris collections. Only Will and I knew there were no plans beyond the meeting with the bishop and leaving the city to take the job offered him at the university in Binghamton at the end of the summer.

He arrived at the chancery office, a formal Victorian building, slightly early for his 11 o'clock appointment. Even though he was deeply assured of his decision, I could feel his tension earlier in the morning, the kind of apprehension that would precede any disagreeable meeting. The first point of entry to the bishop was his secretary, a woman Will had encountered many times. She greeted this priest she had always liked, knowing the purpose of the meeting. "I tried to help her be more comfortable," Will said later. "She's a lovely lady." She led him on to the bishop's next secretary, a priest, a colleague whom Will had known since seminary days and who also, no doubt, was aware of why the meeting was taking place. He was an affable guy and devoted in his mission of serving the bishop. The reverend's secretary was poised, professional and courteous as he led his brother priest to their leader.

Will entered the expansive episcopal office, heading toward this hulk of a muscular man more than six feet tall. He was presiding, not simply sitting in his high-backed executive chair. His salt and pepper hair was topped by his bishop's purple zucchetto. An imposing looking person, he always wore a pince nez and was, this day, in his own version of his business suit – a black vest and waistcoat over his purple rabbet, his jewel-studded gold pectoral cross hanging on his chest, his right hand adorned with a matching gold ring. Will's unadorned black suit was a strikingly humble outfit.

The solemn meeting began. The bishop, his face dark with anger, acknowledged that he had received the letter requesting a leave of absence. "What's the matter, Bill?" he asked, as if the problem were a bad cold.

Will reiterated the contents of his letter, concluding with, "I can no longer represent this organization." After a very brief exchange, which Will could hardly remember, His Excellency moved swiftly and easily to a solution to Will's problems.

Without a flicker of emotion, the bishop asked, "Is there a woman, Bill? Is she pregnant? We can take care of that, you know."

Stunned, Will's response was, "No, Your Excellency. I am not leaving for a woman. I am leaving for the reasons I wrote you. I have too many questions. Mainly, I don't know that this is my path."

His Excellency had recently broken his leg. Leaning on the cane he had propped at the side of his desk, he rose, like the Great White Whale, from his ornate chair, pointed his cane toward the door.

He roared at Will: "Just go!"

THE GOSPEL ACCORDING TO W & M

Will said later that he thought the bishop was going to hit him with his cane. It was rumored that, as Will was leaving the room, the bishop muttered to his secretary, "Maybe if I had made him superintendent he would have stayed."

Will left the office in Brooklyn, never to return to it, never to speak with His Excellency again. He rushed to his Beetle, parked outside the chancery office, drove back over the bridge to Manhattan and, after an intense greeting at my apartment, we took off for the Berkshires. We drove to the old Williams Inn, where we had reserved two rooms, one for Mr. Scanlan and one for Miss Sheehan. Only after we had safely settled in Williamstown did we talk about the day.

It was the first time that a priest in the Brooklyn Diocese had come before this bishop asking for a leave of absence. A few others had left the priesthood, but they had done so without any process or acknowledgement. They just disappeared. It was at dinner that night that Will began musing about the day. "This was an historic day in Brooklyn, Darling," he said as he playfully fed me dessert. He then told me, in his most professorial voice, that it was an earth-shattering moment for His Excellency, a moment of rage, probably also a moment of fear at losing one of his top team members, but primarily one of rage. This was a Prince of the Church, a Protector of the Faith, the former head of Catholic Charities in New York City, a builder, an organizer. He had expanded the high school system significantly in the 1950s and had appointed the thirty-year-old priest to be assistant superintendent of what was to become the largest Catholic high school system in the nation. "I guess he had high hopes for me when he put me in that job," was Will's conclusion.

The next morning at the Inn in Williamstown, I rumpled up the sheets on the bed in my room so that the maid would believe I had slept in that room the night before. We had enjoyed a long leisurely afternoon, a superior meal and a superb concert under the Tanglewood stars. We returned to the city and began charting out the next steps.

As our path revealed itself, time was a mystery to me in 1967. Every day was a minute and a month, a phenomenon I can only attribute to the intensity of my journey. There were no markers, no signposts. There were days when I was on the right course, firm-footed, happy and calm. There were days I slipped and fell by the roadside, discouraged, frightened, sad, unsure of my course, hitting roadblocks.

There was no model for our path. We just kept making decisions as we went along. At Thanksgiving, we announced officially to our universe of family, friends and colleagues that we were going to be married. This was not the initial plan. The initial plan was that Will would go to Binghamton, find out if he liked the work at the university, find out how it felt to live outside the church, find out if he really loved me. I would stay at *Bazaar*, find out how it felt to live without him in New York. My assigned task was much easier on the surface. We would spend a year apart to see if we were really suited to one another.

"I don't know if I can make it in the real world," Will would often say. Although he had held that responsible position in the church school system, although he had successfully managed his financial affairs, he had never really lived alone, never cooked, done laundry, hung pictures on the wall, fixed a running toilet.

"Remember," he nervously joked, "I have consecrated hands," which meant that he couldn't do domestic chores. Aside from in my apartment, he had hardly ever even washed dishes since he was a teenager.

Weekends during the fall of 1967, we would be together. Will would leave Binghamton at the close of the day on Friday and drive to Manhattan. These were intense times, discussing what we were doing, what we were feeling, how we should proceed. Mostly, we talked about Will's work and some vague future plan to be together. My work was a kind of a filler. It was there, rather ignored. I continued to love it but never considered it to be a factor in our decisions.

With the help of his two courageous professional assistants from the Education Office, Sister Mary Thomas and Brother Joseph, Will moved his personal belongings to a furnished apartment in Johnson City close to campus. There were no farewell parties from his fellow priests, no offers of support, nothing but silence from his peers and superiors of more than a decade. He was the bad apple in the barrel, a pariah, an embarrassment. When asked why he chose Binghamton, Will would say that he didn't want to trade on past clerical connections by staying in New York. He realized also that it would be harder to escape his clerical background in the city. He wanted a totally different environment. And then, there was the job offer at the university in Binghamton.

Sister Mary Thomas and Brother Joseph were distraught that their beloved leader was leaving and were themselves confused and frightened by the changes in the church. Sister Mary Thomas, who had a Ph.D. in education, was an expert in curriculum and had a serious concern about the new world of the church. The leadership of her religious order, the Dominicans, had responded to the so-called modernization of the church with a seemingly easy solution. All the women in their order were banned from wearing the traditional habit, which Sister Mary Thomas had worn for twenty years.

"We have to get over our habits," she would jokingly say. But now in her forties, for the first time in her life she would have to bare her head and reveal her body in a way she had not done since she entered the convent. She had to visualize herself as a woman, unwrap her body from its layers of cloth and decide what to wear, whether or not to wear makeup and how to fix her hair. Her concerns about her appearance, her dismay at her appearance, became the focus of her spiritual life. It was so sad.

Brother Joseph, also a highly educated professional, only had to worry about his spiritual life as a Christian Brother and whether or not he wanted to continue the way he had lived since he was an adolescent. Kindly, they put their fears aside for the moment and helped their leader make his move.

After Will's meeting with the bishop and our glorious weekend in the Berkshires, we began telling our good news to friends and colleagues. The story was still in development, but we could let our friends know that Will was leaving Brooklyn, leaving the priesthood and heading for Binghamton; that I was, for the moment, staying at the magazine; that he would see if he could live the life of a lay person, on his own, in an apartment in a little town near the university; that we were an item, we loved each other, and we didn't know yet how our tale would unfold.

After his announcement and the follow-up meeting, he had to leave the rectory as soon as possible. He spent his free days at my apartment, traveling to and from Binghamton as often as possible, even after he found his new home. Playing house a little, I helped him purchase pots and pans, a cookbook (hardly ever opened), sheets and towels, and other necessities of daily life that he had never had to think about. It was fun for me to help a grown man decide such things as how many dishes he would need, what color towels he'd prefer. It was charming to witness his delight in discovering the domestic details of life.

The fun part ended with apartment furnishing. The discomfort and pain part came as we told our story on deeper and deeper levels. The story told, however, was the same for everyone. Friends were the easiest to tell. At first, my friends were shocked by my choice. Each questioned me lovingly and deeply about my motives and desires, and then, returned to friendship and support. Once they met Will and experienced us together, they were comforted by my choice. My magazine colleagues were stunned, incredulous, unable to comprehend my decision. They only knew me in the world of media and high fashion. They didn't really know the little Irish Catholic girl from Queens, the liberal intellectual who was entranced with her love's mind. The men I had dated seemed scornful, angry and suspicious when I told them about Will.

Will's priest friends, his true friends, were happy for him. The other priests were scandalized, outraged, disbelieving. Those colleagues all assumed I was the source of Will's "trouble," that sexual needs had overwhelmed him and driven him to what they perceived as craziness. The easiest news for them would have been that he had fallen in love and had to get married. The most difficult news, the story they, to a man, did not want to hear was that Will could no longer represent the corporation with honesty and integrity.

The most challenging audiences for our tale, of course, were our families. What to tell, how much to tell, when to tell. With great unease we conceived our plot to individually and separately talk to his parents and my parents. All we would tell them at this point was that Will was taking a leave of absence.

The day he received his degree from NYU, he took his parents, Mildred and Maurice, to dinner and told them he was requesting a leave of absence and hoping to find a job somewhere outside of the city. Their response was calm and seemed to be accepting. They knew that he was increasingly unhappy with his priesthood. Maurice, the more religious of his parents, was worried more about Will's soul – and his own – than about his son's prospects for the future. My name was not mentioned in that conversation. His parents were able to put their religious allegiances aside for the sake of the well-being of the son they so loved and adored.

My parents were rather dispassionate when I told them about the priest I had been working with on his thesis. They knew him ever so slightly since he had arranged for my mother to get a teaching position the year before. "He seems like a very nice man," they responded. They never asked questions. He was a priest, an untouchable one, an authority. No questions. But then it was only part of the story.

Each time we successfully told our tale, we rejoiced at acceptance, cried over disapproval or recognized misunderstanding. The month of spreading the news felt like a year. There were days when I was overwhelmed with tears from morning until night, hiding them as much as possible from my colleagues, letting them flow at night alone or talking with my cousin or sister or friend Faith about the details of a given day. Never once did I think of turning back. We were totally unsure of the chapters, fumbling and failing at times, but letting the plot unfold nonetheless. At moments, the tension between us would be so great that we thought our upcoming separation would be a good thing. It was not a good thing. Out last moments together before he took off for Binghamton in the Beetle were so painful that we couldn't speak.

The day after he left was the loneliest one of my life in New York. Sobbing to Faith I begged her, "Let's have dinner together. I can't bear being alone until it's so late I'll just fall asleep." We had dinner at a neighborhood restaurant on Madison Avenue, after which my dear friend walked me home to my apartment, up the three flights of stairs and saw me safely inside. Her worried face told me how I must have been behaving. I promised her I would not do anything except try to sleep. I did finally sleep, only after taking a sleeping medication prescribed to me by my doctor months before. The next morning was no easier, except that I could focus on an exciting project at the office.

THE WELCOME

No matter the circumstances, a priest's resignation was not welcome news – to anyone. There is an estimate that anywhere from five thousand to seven thousand priests in the United States had resigned from the priesthood by 1967. In another ten years, that number would rise to more than twenty-two thousand. Each resignation was a unique and scandalous situation. Communities and families were distraught, often divided, and unsettled by the news that a Man of God was abandoning his calling.

An article in the October 8, 1967 *New York Times* headlined, "Problem of Ex-Priests Growing," cited these reasons why priests leave: "Either they are priest-worker types, who want to get more involved in social action than their superiors allow, or they have lost their faith, their minds or their virginity."

After a summer of job searching with few responses, Will accepted an administrative position with a good salary at Harper College, which was the State University of New York's Binghamton campus. Although it seemed far away, it was a compatible administrative position, director of academic advising, with a good salary and a promising future. Will liked the president and the dean he would be working with and was excited about living in a whole new world.

In the eyes of his friends and family, he had only asked for a leave of absence and was considering his future. His parents had been aware of his unhappiness in the past year or so. "I knew he was confused," his mother would tell me later. "I just thought it was a phase, though, probably because he was working so hard between the office and finishing his degree. I thought he was overtired. Everybody in our parish loved him, and they were always happy when he came to say Mass. He was so good to people."

We had our plan. The leave of absence was Will's careful first step. We discussed every detail so much we thought the plan was foolproof. Marriage was our goal, sooner rather than later. Our original plan to wait a year was scrapped. Being together was the urgent goal. Somehow, I would untangle myself from *Bazaar* and move to Binghamton. No hesitancy on my part. "A new adventure," I thought, never fretting that my career would take a setback once I left Manhattan for wherever-that-place was. I just assumed that my work would speak for itself and carry lots of clout in Binghamton. I never considered that there might not be a substitute for the magazine in a city that had lost its economic base of manufacturing and was struggling to revive itself into who-knew-what.

"Let's find a judge and have a civil wedding ceremony somewhere in the city," Will suggested. "I'll ask Jimmy Regan if he knows anyone who'll do this." We knew that the Vatican wasn't granting dispensations in a timely manner, and Will would have to go through the Vatican process if we were to be married in the Catholic Church. But we didn't care whether or not we were married in the church, and we assumed our loving parents would understand and respect our adult decisions.

Before we had too many wedding plans in place we knew that we'd have to deal with our families. None of them knew of our involvement beyond the fact that we were working together. We had carefully covered up any information about our life together. Since he was no longer living at the rectory, Will had to have a place to stay when he was in New York, other than my apartment. His friend Benito Perry, still a priest, but on the verge of resigning, had an apartment not too far from mine. His telephone number became Will's access number for his parents. Whenever they called the number, Benny would call my apartment and pass the message along to Will. "I hate this deception," Will said to me one night. But we were not quite ready to disclose our situation to family at that point.

Maurice and Mildred were happy that their son was enjoying his work and able to live a healthy and balanced life outside of the priesthood. They were not prepared for his announcement of our love. Will carefully told them that he had not lost his mind, that he loved his new work but that he no longer could function as a priest. Solemnly, he told them, as succinctly as possible, that he really questioned the organization. And then he told them that he had fallen in love with the editor of his thesis. "I haven't yet lost my faith," he explained "but I certainly question it. And this has nothing to do with Mary. As you know, I've been on this path for a couple of years." Choking back tears, he added, "But then I was lucky enough to meet Mary, and that has made more sense to me than anything."

The moment Will left, his mother immediately called her daughter with a famous quote, screeching into the phone, "Billy has a girlfriend!" She then took to her bed. Just as Will had predicted. Her nervous collapse at our announcement was followed by an attack of colitis. Then she rallied, though not enough to offer to meet me. Two weeks later, when we did meet at their home, she emerged from her bedroom and talked to me briefly, with clear discomfort. It was a while before she came to terms with me, but she eventually did, with great drama. Like any diva, she always had to be at center stage. Her discomfort soon passed because she didn't want to lose contact with her son by misbehaving. Within a couple of months, we were having daily telephone conversations about nothing (which continued for the rest of her life).

His father reacted with measured and elegant acceptance. I'm sure he prayed a lot for Will to return to the priesthood. He truly loved and admired Will. And, he was a believer. The day after the family meeting, he called me. He was polite and pleasant and said, "Would you have lunch with me next Saturday so that I can meet you and ask you a few questions?" Although I was frightened, I agreed to meet him at a restaurant on Queens Boulevard. Will had no idea his father had called me. When I told him we were lunching, he became protective and chivalrous, refusing to allow me to meet his father alone. We agreed that I would meet his father first, and he would join us after an hour.

Maurice Scanlan and I had a deep conversation. He was a loving and concerned father wanting to know that his son was not in danger. Looking straight at me from across the table covered with paper place mats, kosher pickles and plastic salt and pepper shakers, he said, "Why do you love my son?" I don't remember my answer. I remember my feelings. I was filled with admiration for this man's loyalty to his son and love of his son, and for his courage in taking this risk of even talking with me. We became dear friends then. In fact, he always called me "Mary Dear." Whatever my responses were, they satisfied Will's father and he became our ally.

I thought all was settled with the Scanlans and, trusting Will's analysis of his mother's behavior, knew that she would come around. "They'll call all the family and let them know, then she'll get lots of attention and we'll be asked for dinner." There was only one kink in that scenario. A week after Maurice and I met, Will's brother Richard called him at Benito's. Will got the message and returned his brother's unusual phone call. He and Richard were not close. Richard was Will's youngest sibling, a constant source of embarrassment and worry to the family until recently. He had gone into recovery, to everyone's great relief, and seemed to be behaving like a responsible adult. It was the responsible adult who called and told Will he wanted to meet with him and his father that day. "In fact," Richard said, "I want you to meet Dad and me in an hour at Constantine's in Jamaica."

I was a wreck when Will told me the story. We were enjoying a leisurely Sunday, which was interrupted by this urgent phone call. "I wonder what they want," Will said. "Maybe Richard wants to beat me up." That statement sent me into mild hysteria as Will left for the meeting. Hours went by. I imagined him bloodied and broken, lying in an alley somewhere in Long Island. Of course, that didn't happen. Richard and Maurice just needed to be reassured by their brother and son that he knew what he was doing, that he loved me enough for marriage, that he was willing to make the commitment. They wanted him to know they loved and supported him. Their concern spoke volumes.

A few days later Maurice called Will with a big idea. With much pride, he told his son he would give him whatever funds were needed to secure a speedy Vatican dispensation from the priesthood. "Just like the Kennedys," Maurice said. "You know – from their marriages and stuff." Dispensation would mean we could be married in a Catholic Church. Nothing would have pleased Maurice more. We demurred as politely as possible, trying not to show this earnest man how repulsed we were by the Vatican's hypocrisy in granting dispensations under any circumstances when they were requested by people of power and influence. Will was not eligible for a dispensation at this point since he hadn't even initiated the process, nor was it clear if the corporation would grant him one. At the time, we had no idea just how complicated a Vatican dispensation would be. Nor did we think we really had to care about a dispensation from the pope.

"Thanks, Pop," Will said. "But we really want to do this right. We don't mind going through all the channels." So Maurice, loving his son and welcoming me into his family, accepted our answer.

THE SHUNNING

It's 2007, forty years later. I struggle to wake from a dream, tossing fitfully. I feel as if I've been dreaming it for a long time. I keep trying to make it end by waking up, but I can't.

My family is gathered at a house. We are all adults on our way to a black-tie event, a concert. The opening piece is a composition by one of my cousins, and we have to be at the hall by 6 p.m.

I am causing problems. I am late because I took a nap. When I awake, everyone is dressed and waiting for me. Mother and Dad are yelling at me, my sister Alice is sarcastically chiding me, my other sister Ann is hiding in the corner of room we are in. My brother is absent.

I can't do anything right. They are waiting and waiting. Dad keeps berating me. I try to make the bed I had slept in and can't. It is a huge bed with many covers and pillows that keep getting jumbled up. Finally, my sarcastic sister Alice comes and takes over straightening up the bed, making a big show of my ineptitude. I go to a closet and retrieve a beautiful plum-colored silk embroidered jacket and a long silk skirt. They are a mess of wrinkles. I take a shower, throw on my underclothes, pulling a run in my stockings as I put them on and then try to find an iron. Not finding one, I grab someone's robe and run to my dear California friend's house, mysteriously next door, where she is taking care of someone's child and preparing a meal. She gives me an iron and ironing board that I almost wreck because I had left food in the pocket of the jacket the last time I had worn it. I iron an old melba toast with something mysterious spread on it into the pocket forever.

In the next scene of my dream I am finally ready. I urge everyone to go ahead to the concert hall and promise to meet them there. I arrive a few minutes later than the rest of the family but in time for the concert. The first thing my father notices is that I have a large not-to-be-missed hickey on my neck. "You are a disgrace," he says.

When I awake, I am overwhelmed with a sadness which, I realize, may never leave me.

After only a few months of living apart in Binghamton and Manhattan, we decided that we would marry in January 1968, during Will's winter break from the university. That wasn't the original, carefully thought-out plan. But the joke between us and to our friends was "We need to get married. Our phone bills are astronomical!" We both enjoyed our work lives, but our hearts were now so closely blended that we could hardly bear living separately.

Concerned about how to approach our parents, we decided that I would talk to my Mother and Dad alone, explain everything and then ask them to meet with Will. We would follow the same procedure with Will's parents. We thought a two-step strategy would be more effective. "Perhaps they won't see us at all if we come together," I said. We approached these meetings as if we were planning a business strategy – dispassionate, tactical and with a clear agenda.

Before talking to my parents, I made the rounds of my siblings, telling them my story. To a person, they each let me know me they would be unavailable and out of town when I met with our parents.

Alice was stunned at my news since I had never disclosed anything to her about Will. "Why didn't you tell me earlier?" she asked, obviously hurt. At this time she was married and had one young child. A devout Catholic, she let me know immediately that she could in no way approve of what I was doing and that I did not have her support. "Keep me out of this," she said when I told her I would be speaking to our parents.

Ann, home from her sojourn in Africa with the Peace Corps, in love with her college sweetheart who was heading off to Vietnam, was entranced with my story and promised her support. However, some event she had planned with her beloved drew her away from being able to be with me that day. I understood her dilemma. "Don't worry about it. I can handle it on my own," I reassured her, disappointed that she couldn't be by my side. I also knew how intimidated she was by the authority of our parents.

Next I had to talk to my brother, who by then was a member of the Capuchin Franciscan Friars, a religious order formed in Italy 1528. Since adolescence, he had been in this order, at a boarding high school and then on to a permanent life with the friars. The word "friar" is derived from the romance languages, a word for "brother." My brother left home to join this "family" of the sons of St. Francis of Assisi, a group renowned as peacemakers and simple, approachable clergy often working among the poor. They are recognized by their long brown robes and the long hood, the *capuche*, for which the order is named. My brother's main task for many years was as tailor to his province of men, single-handedly sewing all the robes and hoods for the friars.

"We need to meet for lunch," I said when I called him. "Can you come to the city? I'll buy. I have something serious to discuss with you."

The only other time I had had a serious conversation with my brother had been a few years earlier. The Capuchins had asked him to take a leave of absence because of undiagnosed physical ailments. After making the rounds of various doctors, he was still suffering back pain, joint pain, headaches and tremors. With some trepidation, I cornered him at home one night and began the conversation.

"Jim," I said, using his birth name rather than his religious name that I refused to ever use. "Have you thought about talking to a psychiatrist about your pains? No one else has really given you any answers. You might not approve of psychiatry, but why not give it a try? It can't hurt, and you might find some relief." Jim agreed to think about this. Since we never discussed emotional issues in our family, I was shocked when he let me make an appointment. I offered to accompany him to the doctor, which he also agreed to. As we drove up to the Park Avenue building where the doctor practiced, my brother turned to me and said, "If you ever discuss this with anyone in our family, I'll deny it and never speak to you again." We went into the office on that note. I waited with surprising apprehension and sadness for my brother to emerge from the office. When he did, he said, "Don't ask any questions. I'm not discussing anything." "OK," I agreed as we got into a cab. "Where can I drop you off? I'm going out for dinner." "Grand Central," he said. He left the cab, and we never again discussed his appointment.

On this second serious and intimate occasion between us, he came to Manhattan, to join me for lunch. I sputtered out my tale of love for Will. Staring at me, his eyes and mouth were cold and hard like a great beast preparing for the attack. He became nasty, sarcastic and moralistic, a man who appeared to be taking pleasure in battering me with his verbal abuse.

"What the hell is the matter with you?" he asked. "You always have to go off and do these crazy things, upsetting Mother and Dad, upsetting all of us. You think you're better than us. You think you have all the answers. You're wrong and stupid and wrong. He's a priest, and he can't belong to you. I want nothing to do with you unless you stop this."

The cruelty of his snarling attack was mean enough for me to leave the restaurant in tears, not caring that he remained at the table, not caring who paid the bill. That was the last of our conversations for a few years to come.

Finally, the Saturday arrived when Will and I had decided it was the day for me to meet with my parents. I don't remember the exact date in the late fall of 1967, but I will never forget the day.

On Friday, Will came to the city from Binghamton for the weekend. I couldn't sleep. I couldn't eat. I couldn't stop fretting all night. We had dinner in our favorite little French restaurant across the street where the staff always fussed over us, let us have the corner table and smiled at us, enjoying our romantic touching and talking.

"I can't finish my food," I whined. "All I can think about is tomorrow."

"Well then, let's go back to your place and talk about it some more," he said.

Cuddling on the couch, we, or rather I, obsessively rehearsed my opening lines to my parents. I tried to imagine the scene and thought I knew how to answer what I naively thought would be any tiny questions. I kidded myself that there would be some disagreement, but that my parents would see how important Will was to me and capitulate, ask to meet with him and work out the details of a wedding. After all, they had met Will casually when he was a priest and liked him. I kept turning all of this over in my mind, reviewing all my thoughts and fears with Will. He was so patient. Finally, the only comfort was to end the conversation and make love, passionate, powerful, with no hint of my fear in it. We held on to each other all night in my tiny bed, entwined securely in each other's arms.

The next morning, my stomach was still too full of jumbles for breakfast. Will went out to the bakery and picked up some Danish pastry. I, unable to break routine, had a couple of cups of coffee with my cigarettes, pumping up my adrenaline even more. Dreading the clock as the moments seemed to race by, I finally got in the shower and dressed for the occasion. "Something simple and conservative," I thought. "That dark gray skirt and sweater, not black, not too New Yorky. Easy on the makeup, no perfume."

Keeping the mode conservative, I decided to take the bus across the bridge and over to Queens, promising myself a cab ride back to the city. The bus was fairly empty as it lumbered across the bridge. I carefully studied the faces around me and wanted to stand up and say, "Do any of you know what I'm doing? Do you think I'm a bad girl? Would you still love me if I were your daughter?"

Irrational thinking had taken over fear during the ride. I was envisioning the Scarlet A that I imagined my parents would slap on my chest. By the time I had walked the few streets from the bus stop to my parents' apartment building, I felt strong, although I could feel my body shaking as I rode the elevator to the fourth floor. My mother unlocked three bolts slowly and opened the door. "Hello, Dear," she said flatly and without any warmth or enthusiasm, giving me her usual cool peck on the cheek. I was never allowed to kiss her on the lips. Nor to give her a hug. She always turned her head to offer a high-boned cheek.

Dad was reigning in his living room leather chair, the one that was always reserved for him and that no one sat in when he wasn't there. He gave me a big and strong hug and a juicy kiss, even though he didn't get up from his chair. His "Hello, Dear" was booming and energetic.

I had only told them I was coming for a short visit. I don't know if they wondered about it or just accepted it as one of my Saturday excursions. They had so little information about my life, only absorbing whatever stories I offered about life at the magazine. Every once in a while my father would ask me about men he thought I might still be dating or about my work with Father Scanlan on his thesis. But it had been a number of years since I had told them about anything in my life that was important to me when I knew I would meet with their disapproval.

It was, indeed, a very short visit. We sat in their living room, my mother on the turquoise sectional sofa adjacent to my father's chair, I facing them both from a marigold yellow wing chair. "I have some news," I said.

Dad made a joke of some kind, as was his way when anything that sounded serious was introduced. I reminded them of Father Scanlan, the priest with whom I had worked, the priest who had procured a teaching position for Mother when she foolishly thought she wanted to work after being at home for thirty years.

"Well, remember I told you he had left the priesthood. He's been living in Binghamton, working at the university, and we are going to be married. When would you like to meet with him?"

So much for the rehearsed speech! It probably took me sixty seconds to get all of that out before I took a second breath. Dad started battering me with questions.

"What do you mean, he left the priesthood? What about his vows -- once a priest always a priest? Why have you been lying to us and sneaking around about this. When did this start? How could you do this to us? This is going to kill me!"

Mother became a stone. She said nothing. After a few minutes of shouting, Dad exploded, "Get out now!" Mother said nothing.

I asked for mercy. I asked for understanding. I told them I loved them and wanted no harm to come to them. I told them I loved Will, and I would be marrying him no matter what. Dad was now sobbing and bellowing at the top of his voice at the same time, condemning me, cursing me. Mother was ice -- silent, condemning. The shunning had begun.

It's an ancient religious tradition, this shunning thing. Not only the Catholic Church, but Jews, Anabaptists, Amish, Mormons and

Jehovah's Witnesses also have traditions of ostracizing and exiling individuals. Shunning can be substantiated by some biblical teachings and has been practiced by some sects, although not all scholars or denominations agree on the interpretations of the verses.

In I Corinthians 5:11-13, it's written: "But now I am writing you that you 'must not associate' with anyone who calls himself a brother but is sexually immoral or greedy, an idolater or a slanderer, a drunkard or a swindler. With such a man, do not even eat. What business is it of mine to judge those outside the church? Are you not to judge those inside? God will judge those outside. Expel the wicked man from among you." Verses from Matthew, Thessalonians, Romans and John have also been cited to substantiate shunning.

My parents had no biblical verses to recite, no institutional rule to reference. When we met, I had broken no church law. Yet fear, embarrassment and shame drove them to an extreme religious tradition. For the next three years, in spite of my wonderful new life with Will, I was tortured by one thought, "How could a mother and father, but especially a mother, reject her child for an institution?" Their answer: their daughter, the whore, had seduced a holy man who had promised himself to God.

AFTER SHUNNING

I left my parent's apartment with my stomach in a knot and my heart seared and broken. I know I was crying, but it was that kind of crying that you can't even notice because you're so immersed in your sadness. My fear was gone, my strength was sapped. I slowly walked towards Queens Boulevard to hail a cab over the bridge and back to my nest. I couldn't wait to see Will. No, I couldn't wait to collapse in Will's arms, to have him comfort me and help me sort out what had just happened. I didn't really know what had just happened with my mother and father. I could understand it if my parents were surprised, upset, confused and angry. I expected that. I couldn't understand stone-cold silence from my mother and the raging banishment from my father.

Will was waiting. His "How'd it go?" set me into heaving sobs. Between those sobs, I told him about the scene. Even as I was telling him I couldn't believe some of the things my parents said to me.

"They'll get over it," he said. "They just need time. They're shocked and confused. But you know they love you and they'll come around. They're good people." Those comments were such a reflection of Will's faith in people. He always wanted to think the best of everyone. He always said, "Everyone does their best." He sounded so sure of himself that I began to believe I'd be talking to my parents soon again.

The shunning silence was broken only by the early morning phone calls from my father. He began a barrage of these calls, questioning my mental health, asking what I planned to do to change my life, anxiously awaiting, I supposed, a retraction and a confession of wrong. The formal enforcement came when my mother called a couple of weeks later to remind me to come to Thanksgiving dinner. "I'll only come if I can bring Will," I responded. "Oh no, Dear," she said. "You just come alone, and we won't talk about it." Taking a long hard breath, I said, "I can't do that, Mother." She hung up the phone firmly. It would be the last conversation for almost three years. No more early morning phone calls, no more invitations to any family events, no more trying to convince me of the error of my ways.

Word started coming back to me through my loyal sister Ann that my large family was being notified of my transgression. "I was at Bobby Gaughan's engagement party," said Ann, "and he said, 'I hear you and your sister are both getting married, but that nobody's going to Mary's wedding.'" Then a friend from the old neighborhood, who had gone to elementary, high school and college with me, called. I hadn't spoken to Christine in a while because our lives were on very different paths. "What's going on?" she demanded in her usual street tough way. "I met your mother on the street and asked how you were and she said, 'We don't talk about Mary. We don't approve of her.' What the hell does that mean?" Christine knew nothing about my life with Will, so it was a long conversation. She was still a practicing Catholic, but she was also a practicing psychologist. She was curious, titillated, and supportive of her old chum from first grade. She became the bearer of the tale to my school friends.

The stunning revelation to me was that everyone in my family was talking about me and nobody was talking to me. Well, not quite everybody. My sister Ann and my cousin Mary, who had introduced Will and me, were at my side, available day and night as I sorted through my emotional responses to the situation. I expected shock from my professional friends and colleagues. In my naiveté, I certainly never expected the extreme reaction from my family. My parents had somehow terrorized most of the rest of the relatives. No one dared contact me in person. I received mail from one aunt, who wrote, "Although I'm not Catholic, I believe that if 'he' broke one set of vows (priesthood), he'll probably break another (marriage)." My godparents, whom I adored, were silent, stalwart in their role of defending the faith. My beloved Aunt Peg was brokenhearted. She invited me to meet her for dinner one evening in November, at Gage and Tollner's in Brooklyn, near where she lived. I took the subway to that elegant landmark. When I arrived, I knew at once that she had already had a drink or two to fortify her for our dinner. By the end of the meal, alcohol had overwhelmed her. Tearfully and with slurred speech, she handed me an envelope, she said, "You know I love you, but my church won't let me come to your wedding. This is for you. I want to be there, but I can't." It was such sadness for me to see her in this dilemma. At least I knew how she felt about me. I understood her conflict with her church and my mother, her sister.

The big delight was Aunt Ceal, my mother's youngest sister. She and Peg had been the two aunts who snuck towels and dishes and other household necessities to my new apartment when my parents disapproved of my living arrangements. Ceal had married for the first time when she was in her fifties. She was an executive secretary in a large construction company, the kind of executive secretary that everyone today wishes they had, the kind who ran the company in reality.

She met Wes when she started working there and, when his wife died they started seeing each other. He was in his sixties, an accountant and the purchasing agent for the company. A descendant of American colonial settlers and conservative in his appearance, he drove a Jaguar, which charmed my aunt no end. They were married by one of our cousins who was a priest, but the ceremony had to be outside the church altar because Wes was Protestant. In those days, Catholics who married baptized non-Catholics could not be married on the altar. When Ceal and Wes heard from my mother that I was marrying someone she didn't approve of, Wes, in defiance of his sister-in-law, whom he called "Queenie," was quoted as saying, "Ceal, invite them over here. We can't abandon Mary." Ceal, delighted with the opportunity to stand up to her imposing oldest sister, was furious at Queenie in the situation. Soft-spoken but firm, buttressed by her darling man's conviction, she called me and invited us for dinner to meet Will and "talk about things."

Will and I drove to Teaneck for our dinner with Aunt Ceal and Uncle Wes. He and Will became immediate pals. We talked about our unfolding plans, and everything was very civilized. Both of them made it crystal clear to us that they believed my parents were behaving badly and that we deserved family support. They were at our disposal. They would be my surrogate parents. We could ask them for anything. They didn't care where the wedding took place. They were there.

THE HEALER

I am reminded of the Gospel stories in which Jesus comforted the dying, healed and anointed the sick of heart and body, accepted the unacceptable. For Will and me, Joseph Duell Sullivan was a model of that very model healer.

Three years before we met, Father had searched for a healer, someone who could help him understand whether or not he was losing his mind. "All my life," he said to me later, "the only thing I had ever wanted to do was be a priest or a monk. And then, after thirteen years as a priest, I began questioning everything about this life." Given his family's history of mental illness and this enormous shift in his thinking, he decided he needed professional help.

"I didn't want to load the dice in my favor," Will said. "I didn't want to get help from someone who would easily tell me to resign from my priesthood." Rather than choose a liberal Jewish Freudian psychoanalyst, he chose an Irish Catholic psychiatrist. Assuming he would find a like-minded person familiar with the church and its issues, Father consulted the Catholic Charities directory to find his man. Dr. Sullivan, a mild-mannered redhead, about Will's age, although he was not, of course, a priest, practiced in a Manhattan office and was a referring doctor for Catholic Charities in the New York Archdiocese.

Will went to Dr. Sullivan for counseling on a regular basis from 1965 until 1967. Since he chose to do this on his own rather than being sent by his bishop for counseling, he paid the fees from his own pocket.

He worked with Dr. Sullivan on his concerns about his priesthood and his sanity until they got to the point where the doctor assured him he was sane and told him he needed to leave the priesthood. While Will and I were working on his thesis, he was still seeing Dr. Sullivan, but telling me after many meetings, "I really helped Dr. Sullivan today," meaning that they had come to a point where the healer was talking to the patient about his own problems with the Catholic Church. They had become friends and colleagues, united in mind about the current state of affairs in the Catholic Church.

I met Dr. Sullivan shortly after I told my parents that Will and I were going to marry. My father decided that, among other things, I was emotionally unbalanced. That was when he began making those 7 a.m. phone calls. Each morning Dad exhorted, "Have you changed your mind about marrying that man?" When I demurred, he exploded with rage and accusations. After a few weeks of these wrenching conversations and my unwillingness to comply with his demands, he burst out, "I think you're mentally ill." Although I was becoming used to his abusive accusations, I was shocked that my father would even suggest mental illness.

Mother always said, "We won't talk about it," when referring to anyone who might be suffering from any emotional problem. Mental illness was never considered a possible explanation for any family member's deviant behavior. It was as if our family was immune to it. I asked Dad if he thought I should see a doctor. When he said yes, I suggested Dr. Sullivan, whom I forthrightly described as Will's psychiatrist. He paused, and then agreed that he would accept a diagnosis and any recommendation from Dr. Sullivan. After all, the doctor had a good Irish name.

Even though I had heard Will's stories about this healer, I was apprehensive going to his office, afraid that he might see me as a Jezebel or that he might tell me I was out of my mind and that I should end the relationship. I had had limited experience with mental health practitioners. I found myself in the care of a man of profound morality, a believer in the unity of mind and body, clear and certain in his speech, kind and warmhearted.

In three sessions he and I discussed my family, my religious beliefs and my feelings for Will. Then Dr. Sullivan said, "In our next session I'd like Will and you to come together so we can talk more about your relationship."

We drove to his office tense and hardly speaking, not knowing what the outcome would be. We waited in the anteroom of his office suite until he warmly greeted us. He invited us in to his private office and asked us to sit together on a beige couch facing his desk. Instead of presiding from behind a desk, he sat in an upholstered office chair facing us.

With measured speech, he summarized for us his opinion of the strength of our relationship. It was clear to me from his remarks that he was fond of Will and respectful of his decision. "Your parents are frightened, dismayed and embarrassed, Mary. They are locked in the arms of the church," he said. "They are unable to approve of your behavior since the church has declared it was scandalous and sinful. You two know what you're doing. Keep going." And then he said, "Have your parents come see me, Mary." His words will forever ring in my ears. Only after he said that did he smile. He then hugged us both as we, with tears running down our faces, gathered ourselves together to leave this healing place.

I quoted that statement to Dad with a certain glee mixed with fear of his reaction. He said nothing. In our next early morning conversation, I asked him when he and Mother would be meeting with Dr. Sullivan. Acting surprised or annoyed, he said, abruptly, "We won't be doing that." My parents could not take the risk of discussing the situation with a relatively objective person. I was hurt that my work with Dr.

Sullivan had been dismissed. I realized I was at an impasse with my parents.

However, I was elated with Dr. Sullivan's "diagnosis." I don't know if he ever realized that he had healed me from any hesitation I had about continuing my relationship. His boundless support was the cure.

PLANNING, PLANNING, PLANNING

Once settled in Johnson City, Will had the support of an administration colleague from the university, who took him to the local bank to introduce him to his banker, escorted him around the campus to meet colleagues, shared his family's time and affection with him and listened to Will's story. Although he tried to keep the past secret, word leaked out about the priest who was working on campus, and Will became an unwilling and uncomfortable source of much curiosity.

His life, however, was not connected to Binghamton. His life was in New York. Almost every Friday afternoon, he would get in the Beetle, hit Route 17 and head to the city, doing the reverse trip Monday at 5 a.m., arriving on campus for his first 9 o'clock meeting of the day. I flew to Binghamton a couple of times to spare him the trip. I was not very impressed with Johnson City or Binghamton's rust belt appearance and mentality. The university was dynamic, but the surrounding area was gray and depressing. However, we played house when I visited him. I cooked all our meals and helped organize his apartment, and we explored the nearby neighborhoods. When he came to New York we became embroiled in serious, serious discussions about our future and tried to have a little fun in between those discussions.

I was ready to move forward in a life with Will. He was worried about his ability to succeed outside religion, unsure that he could support my lifestyle. One night in New York we celebrated with a dinner date at the Maisonette Café at the St. Regis Hotel where Julie Wilson was performing. It was a romantic evening until the walk back to my apartment. As we rounded the corner on Madison Avenue, a glum-looking Will said, "I can't afford you, and I'm too uncomfortable in your world." Dumbstruck, I asked what he meant. He told me he was afraid that the Maisonette club life was where I belonged and that I would be unhappy with anything else. "Living with me in a place that's far, far from here," he said, "will never work for you. And I'll never make the kind of money to support a life like this." That night never ended. We talked this conflict out into the next morning until we assured each other we were on the same path.

Our love for each other was never an issue. We continued to marvel at how similar our thinking was on matters of importance to us. How did we ever get to the same place about religion from such different paths at such different times in our lives? How did we come to love the same kind of music before we had met? How did we each know when laughter could soothe a tough situation, calm an anxious moment and open a door? We came to believe we were soul mates before we ever came together. We tortured each other with the intensity of our conversations. We had no role models and no compass, but we were both used to being decision makers who tried to consider every inch of an issue before proceeding.

As the days between the weekends became more miserable, I gave Will an ultimatum. He had to make a decision to marry me or not within six months. Never in my young life had I been focused on marriage. It was something out there that I expected would happen, but I had not been in a rush. That was no longer the case. I wanted a decision from this man. If I couldn't be with him, I had to know that soon. I had to end the torment I was experiencing.

I was never privy to his decision-making process, but within a very few weeks, the plan to wait a year was discarded. We decided to push a wedding date to the coming January while Will was on winter break.

Unbeknownst to me, Will and my cousin Mary had been conspiring on an engagement ring. She had our grandmother's engagement ring from 1900. She and Will decided that a copy of it would be appropriate. Will took the ring to a jeweler in Binghamton and arranged to have a copy made to present to me at Thanksgiving. I was so thrilled with this sentimental plot. With that ring I was bonded to my family in a symbol of tradition if nothing else. We had our first lovely Thanksgiving weekend, alone in a city that was practically deserted after the Thanksgiving Day Parade. The streets around my apartment were empty, seemingly available only to the two of us, blissed out on love and romance.

Now we had to figure out how and where to have a wedding.

THE MIRACLE WORKER

In general, a miracle in the Catholic tradition is defined as a wonderful thing. The word stems from the Latin *micrari*, meaning to wonder. A miracle is a wonder performed by supernatural powers as a sign of some special mission or gift and explicitly ascribed to God.

My friend Faith is a person of wonder. Appropriately named, she is a woman of faith with an abiding belief in her blended values, neither stuffy nor pompous about her faith, living it in her relationships.

We met in the '60s, as I mentioned earlier, when we were two young women working as editorial assistants at *Harper's Bazaar*. She was in the editorial department and I in the promotion and merchandising department. Miraculously, we lived one street away from each other – she on 68th Street, just off Madison Avenue and I on 67th on Madison. A woman of wit and intelligence and sophistication, she was a graduate of Smith College, an English major like me. We were drawn to each at first by misery in the workplace and then by the joy of getting to know each other. We both lived alone – I in my little nest, she in a more splendid grown-up apartment – and shared meals on a regular basis, along with stories of work and family and love. We both smoked and worried constantly about being thin enough (by *Harper's Bazaar* standards), constantly experimenting with new diet plans or clothes that would make us look thinner or hair that would make us look thinner or makeup that would make us look thinner. We also did our marketing together on Saturdays, schlepping a joint shopping cart filled with empty returnable soda bottles, from Madison Avenue to the supermarket on Lexington Avenue. Once there, we would march up and down the aisles looking for bargains. Under Faith's tutelage I learned about shopping for store brands and buying the specials of the week, always looking for a bargain. Although our weekends were spent in different worlds of family and boyfriends, we spent free weeknights verbally churning work and love and family issues with great angst.

Even though she knew every secret of my heart, I was uncomfortable telling Faith about Will. I don't know when I finally did confess, but I do know she was immediately supportive and became even more so when others were skeptical, critical or condemning. Everything was happening so quickly. The complexities of our getting married seemed so enormous. Faith, in the most caring and kind manner, must have recognized that and had an idea right away. "I'll take care of the wedding," she said. "Just leave all the details to me and you can focus on everything else." It was such a generous offer, but I would have to consult with Will about it. We three had dinner.

Faith had such faith in Will and me. So much so that she startled her own family with her offer of helping us make a wedding. We were not in their social or economic or religious circle. I think I had only been to her family's estate in Greenwich once before we were married and met only her mother and grandmother at that time. Her much-loved grandfather and her impressive father were never present when I was with her. The family wasn't too sure who Will and I were and, although we never discussed it, I would guess they were skeptical about her generous offer.

That offer was not well received at first by Will. It was too much generosity for him to accept, and he had a certain pride to maintain. By the end of dinner, we agreed to share the wedding expenses and the workload. Faith would make all the arrangements for the celebration after the ceremony. She would transform her beautiful apartment, arranging the space, decorating it appropriately. She and I would decide on the food. She would hire a caterer. Will and I would take care of whatever kind of ceremony we could conjure up. We would do all the invitations and take care of our wedding garments and the gifts for our bridal party.

It was all so bizarre and frenetic. It was wonderful and scary. Faith was my touchstone to sanity through it all. The path between our apartment doors was well worn long before the wedding. As January 1968 approached, her doorman knew me well enough that he didn't even have to ask who I wanted to see and would simply smilingly buzz me up.

Some nights I would arrive at her apartment and cry. Cry because I, like most brides, wanted my mother to be part of my planning, cry because I would have just had yet another bitter exchange with yet another member of my family, cry because I was frightened, emotionally exhausted and unsure of myself from time to time. Faith would talk me through my upheaval, keep me on track and offer the healing touch I needed.

We chose the date, a Wednesday in January. It was another symbol. Father and I had always worked together on his thesis on Wednesdays, and then Will and I always met for dinner or movies or theater on Wednesdays. We began the search for the official to perform the ceremony. Will was in charge of that and decided to confer with his clergy friends to find the right person.

Faith and I set about choosing invitation paper, ink, typeface – all the things we had learned at the magazine. Even without the officiator, we knew we had to get the invitations sent out quickly. Of course, we went to Tiffany's and they produced a beautiful invitation. Because everything we were doing was unconventional, there was even an unconventional twist to the invitation. We invited people in two categories: those who were totally open to our marriage were invited to the ceremony and the reception; those who would feel compromised in any way by the civil ceremony were invited to the reception only. This group included our families and any of Will's priest and nun friends who were supportive. We were concerned about not offending anyone, and we tried to take every person's beliefs into account.

Invitations under control, Faith and I then turned to the reception. At this point, Faith took over, clarified our preference for food and promised to let me know when she had made all the arrangements for food and drink, cake, flowers and furniture. At the same time, she was becoming more involved with a man she decided she wanted to marry. In the midst of preparations for our wedding, she became engaged and her parents decided to throw an engagement party for her. I worried about her ability to focus on her news and be our miracle worker at the same time. But she assured me she had everything under control for our event. I trusted her taste without question, so that I could leave the details of the reception aside while we struggled with a ceremony, leaving my job at *Bazaar*, finding an apartment in for us Binghamton, arranging my move from New York and dealing day after day with the drama of our story.

Robert Day-Dean's

FIVE EAST FIFTY-FOURTH STREET

NEW YORK, N.Y. 10022   (212) 755-8300

CATERING
DEPARTMENT

December 22, 1967

Miss Mary Sheehan
Harpers Bazaar
572 Madison Avenue
New York City

Dear Miss Sheehan:

We are pleased to submit an estimate for
the Wedding Reception on January 17, 1968, after the
12:30 service in an apartment on East 68th Street.

Based on an attendance of 50 persons,
the price on the menus include all food and equipment.
Additional items will be as follows:

One Bartender, Two Butlers and One Pantry Woman - $30. each
Bridal Cake, 8-12, Orange filling   - $40.00

It is understood that only champagne will
be served.

Please call us if there are any questions.

Very truly yours,

Edgar D. Hoagland

Edgar D. Hoagland

EDH:VL

A minimum guarantee of the number of guests must be given a week before the function. This guarantee may be increased but not decreased, up to 24 hours before the function at which time the guarantee as to number shall be deemed final. Our charge will be based on the number of guests guaranteed; or, if the total exceeds the number guaranteed, the total will be charged for. This contract is contingent upon the inability of the management to complete the same because of strikes, accidents or other causes beyond its control.

WEDDING GARMENTS

When the time came to decide what we would wear to our wedding, I became intrigued with biblical lore and learned that, in both the Old and New Testaments, garments have symbolical significance, especially wedding garments. In the book of Revelation, God clothes the righteous in the wedding garment of salvation, saying "the fine linen is the righteous acts of the saints." In other parts of the Old Testament, the white garment is the symbol of a member of the community of the redeemed, and nakedness is a symbol of living in sin. And in the Gospel of Matthew, there is the story of the wedding feast where the king examines all the people from the street who have been invited to his wedding to see if they are wearing the proper wedding garments. One man without a wedding garment is cast out of the party into the darkness. This has been interpreted as a metaphor for Judgment Day, when the unworthy will be banished from the church and the kingdom of God because they didn't perform the good deeds necessary for Christian life and the kingdom.

Will and I knew we needed to take the symbolic step of purchasing special garments for our wedding. Will's wardrobe was still pretty sparse – lots of black socks, black shoes, black suits, lots of casual wear, especially Bermuda shorts, and only the beginnings of a collection of ties and professional suits for work. He wanted a new and distinctive wedding suit. Taking one of his weekend visits to New York as the opportunity to decide on his wedding garments, we went to a venerable men's store, Paul Stuart, on Madison Avenue and 45th Street, and chose a handsome double-breasted dark blue suit, French cuffed shirt and blue and red tie and new black socks. Even though he had black shoes and socks, it was important for Will to buy new black socks and a new pair of black wedding shoes. Which he did. He was all set. In one of my many lists for the event, I noted that we picked up Will's suit with its alterations on Tuesday, the day before the wedding.

My wedding garment was a little more complicated. I agonized over what to wear. For some reason or other, I didn't involve any of my fashion magazine friends and colleagues. I remember wanting to decide about my garment on my own, but feeling very lonely about that prospect at the same time. I didn't want anything formal since the wedding was at noon on a weekday. I wanted something simple and elegant and white – a wedding garment symbolizing a celebration and beauty and marriage. Our wedding date, January 17, 1968, was fast approaching. I couldn't find what I wanted, or didn't really know what I wanted. Anxiety and depression crept in as I ran around bridal salons hating the "Queen for a Day" garments and not knowing where else to turn.

In a mild panic one day in late December, I left the office on my lunch break and walked a few blocks to Saks Fifth Avenue where I found my dress hanging on a rack. It was a street length (actually above the knee) heavy silk coat-style dress with a deep ruffle from neck to hem, which softened its austere lines, and long sleeves ending in the same ruffle. One of the wonderful saleswomen at Saks suggested I change the buttons nestled in the ruffle to make the dress even more special. After purchasing the dress, I went to the famous button shop on Madison Avenue and bought a dozen pearl cluster buttons. They cost almost as much as the dress! Later that week, dress and buttons went to Ann Stalling, who took my wedding garment, adjusted it where necessary and replaced the original twelve buttons with the gorgeous pearl clusters. I also bought a new pair of short white kid gloves and white silk shoes with a pointy toe and two-inch heel.

What to wear on my head was a big concern. No veil for me! I was adamant about that even though nobody had asked me to wear one. My cousin Mary stepped into the headdress situation and offered to make a headpiece from various ribbons. I loved the idea. There was a terrific French ribbon shop not very far from my office. I stopped in, described the dress and the ribbon specialists helped me choose white velvet, grosgrain and silk ribbons and a comb, which Mary fashioned into a headpiece the night before the wedding.

I loved it. And I loved my entire wedding garment. I felt very special in it. If garments signified spiritual good deeds in the Bible and purity of heart, I felt I was in the midst of a wonderful moment of glory and commitment, true to my heart, performing a good deed.

With the reception under control in Faith's good hands, I turned my attention to the other details. Lists piled on top of lists as I wrestled with family issues, clothing issues, work issues, moving issues. And through it all – which was really only less than a two-month period – angels, led by my guardian angel cousin Mary, and Faith at her side, kept swooshing down to guard us, assist us, encourage us.

CHOIR OF ANGELS

By the beginning of December, miraculously, all invitations were mailed. We could manage only fifty people in Faith's apartment. The list had to be carefully compiled, not to offend, not to omit, not to include. Even though there was now a hopeless impasse with my parents, we sent invitations to both sets of parents, all of our siblings and their spouses, aunts and uncles. Then the list extended to our closest friends. That was the toughest group.

We knew we could invite more than we could hold since only my aunt and uncle and one sister were attending from my family. My dear Aunt Peg, sister to my Mother and Aunt Ceal, wrote me a note upon receiving our invitation: "My heart was indeed scalded by the news. It has been my hope that when this occasion finally arrived it would be one of great joy and happiness for you and for us in sharing it. The pain comes in seeing you arrive at it under great difficulties. However, do not shut me out of your life for my love and prayers are with you always. We will get together, but I must have a little more time."

The same day, December 3, 1967, her sister Ceal wrote me: "My faith in you and your integrity is absolute and unquestionable. We will be very happy to help you in any way we can and hope you will give us the privilege of doing so." Help me and us she and Uncle Wes did, becoming my stand-in parents proudly and generously.

Our matron of honor would be my cousin Mary, the very one who had introduced us two years earlier. Her special friend, Lyn, would be our best man. That was a complicated situation since he was attached to my cousin but married to someone else. Mary called me every day to check in on my sanity, kept us all laughing when things became too grim and lovingly supported me like a big sister. Lyn and Will talked from time to time, but Lyn's life was too complex to provide day-to-day support for Will. That was done by his closest friend, Father Tony Antinello, and by Father Jim Regan. Jimmy wanted to perform the ceremony himself but would risk too much in his career to commit what was considered an illegal act in the eyes of the church. Both he and Tony accepted our wedding invitation gleefully. Jimmy went to work and found a judge who was willing to marry us, willing to defy the church and to risk his reputation. His name was Amos Basil, notorious for his liberal tendencies which had recently been contradicted by his role in the closing of the Broadway play "Oh! Calcutta!" for indecency. I never spoke to him before the wedding. There was a ridiculous and annoying part of me that felt like a criminal. The church had done a great job instilling rules and regulations in my head and heart and, while I didn't believe in its principles, there was always a nagging little voice in my head that told me we were sinning. Will was much more comfortable meeting with the judge and discussing our vision for the wedding.

It didn't ever occur to us to write our own personal vows. We were happy with the traditional marriage vows, excluding the promise to obey. We expected the judge to add his personal remarks. We all agreed that the judge would be at Faith's place at 11:30 a.m., we would have the ceremony at noon and reception at 12:30. Timing was important. We meticulously coded the invitations "c" and "r," indicating which people would come to the ceremony as well as the reception and those who would be there for the reception only. We didn't want any of our guests who might be offended or scandalized by the ceremony to come before the reception. Will's parents, for example, were anxious to come but couldn't bring themselves to attend the ceremony because it would have been classified as a sin if they did.

Will's assistants in the superintendent's office agreed to come to the wedding. They had been so helpful to Will in his move to Binghamton and were caught up in the romance and excitement of our drama. Will's brother and sister-in-law accepted our invitation, but his sister and her husband planned a vacation in the Caribbean. Will's parents would attend. My parents continued their silence. My sister Ann, who would attend, of course, was such a pal, but she was scared all the while of our parents' reactions. My sister Alice felt she needed to support our parents and agreed that it would be a sin to attend. My brother declined. Aunts and uncles and cousins were kind and thoughtful, sending us gifts and expressions of encouragement. Everyone in the family was confused. Our invited friends were all coming.

TO DO, RE DO, UN DO –
BEFORE I DO

This must have been the time of my life when I really learned about lists. Even with the Choir of Angels hovering over me, I was on a high cloud those four weeks before our wedding. Appearing to have everything under control, I was a bundle of nerves, hardly sleeping, plagued by worry about some level of detail in one or another segment of life that I might forget or offend.

The lists looked something like this:

20 December 1967

License: Send conviction stub and keep license

Telephone: Call representative so that you can give him notice of when you want telephone disconnected and to give him your final billing address

Social Security: Send in application for name change

Voting: Re-register in Binghamton. Say that you voted under your maiden name in New York

Con Edison: Cancel services as of 1/18/68

Another list stated:

All clothes from cleaner. Tiffany for envelopes. Mail fabric. Turn off telephone. Get keys to Mr. Selwyn. Tip for Manuel. Deliveries from Vanity Fair and Monteil. Insurance policy. Arrangements for bed. Ann Stalling to fix hems. WGS clothes from Paul Stuart.

In a word – or words – that list reminded me to take care of details in my apartment with the landlord and the porter, to arrange for gifts that I was supposed to be receiving be sent to me in Binghamton, to be sure our new bed was delivered to the right apartment in Binghamton, along with the drapery fabric, and to take care of the last minute details of our wedding garments.

Then there were the lists for Faith's apartment for the ceremony and reception, and for the ultimate countdown lists for Monday, Tuesday and Wednesday of the week we were getting married: Where in Faith's apartment would the ceremony be held? Where would the wedding cake be placed? What about coat racks? What kind of money did we need to take care of for food and Champagne and the judge and the servers and the flowers? And, and, and ...

All the details became increasingly and suddenly important the weekend before the wedding. Faith, a bundle of energy, was someone who paid meticulous attention to detail. Because of that great gift of hers, I was relieved that I didn't have to think about the reception. I trusted her judgment totally and didn't really discuss many of the details once we decided on the menu. Since we were to have a Wednesday noon ceremony, we decided to keep the reception simple and elegant. Champagne would be the only beverage. The menu would be light French food that would be passed by two butlers. There would be a cake with orange filling. There would be one pantry woman to take care of things in the kitchen. The caterer would supply any equipment we needed. All was in Faith's competent and tasteful hands.

Somewhere in the midst of our planning, Faith announced she was going to marry the following summer. We were thrilled for her. We had met Paul once. He had come into Faith's life rather suddenly and, just as suddenly, she decided to marry him. The family was happy for her and planned a party in her honor the Saturday before our wedding. We were unable to attend, embroiled as we were in our own planning and packing and partying.

Late Sunday afternoon, three days before our wedding, Faith's mother called to tell me that her daughter was in the hospital after an accident the night before at her engagement party. Her leg was badly broken. She was in the Guggenheim Pavilion at Mount Sinai Hospital, heavily sedated and unable to communicate. Faith's mother knew that we were being married at her daughter's and that she needed to do something about the use of Faith's apartment but wasn't quite sure what. Could she and I meet there on Monday and go over details?

I was wracked with anxiety, worried about my friend and panicked about my wedding. "When can I see Faith?" I asked her mother. She wasn't sure, but I could call the hospital on Monday, the next day. I did and was told Faith could have visitors later in the day. That night, I met her mother and her grandmother, a formidable duo, at Faith's apartment. Aunt Ceal came with me. It was a very tense scene. The family didn't really know what we were up to.

I had met Faith's mother only once and wasn't inclined to be warm and friendly with her since I had been told many tales about her difficult relationship with her

THE GREAT ALLELUIA DAY

It was a cold, snowy and gray day, not looking like much of a day to celebrate. But in my heart, January 17 was warm and golden, and I was singing "All My Lovin" with joy.

Cousin Mary had spent the night before with me. Although I found her to be annoying as all get-out, I really needed her management skills and her attention to detail. I was buzzing around the apartment, fussing with one detail, turning to another, finding an item I was looking for and then losing it. I was terrified, I was sentimental, and I was exhausted in my recovery from a ten-day battle with the flu and continuous work at the magazine.

My publisher, not happy that I was leaving, decided at the last minute that I couldn't end my days at *Harper's Bazaar* on Friday, that he needed me to be with him at a breakfast fashion show on Monday, two days before our wedding. I argued with him about it, but he was adamant, and I had not yet learned how to say no to an employer.

I was excited. I was determined. I was wrapped in a gauzy coat of love. On Tuesday night I talked endlessly with Mary about my hopes for my future, never acknowledging even to myself – my apprehensions about moving the next day to an unfamiliar community and a whole new life. We read poetry to each other and finally slept for a little while.

I arose early to have my hair arranged by Antonio, the hairdresser who conveniently had a salon on the first floor of my building. Mary had sewn together the ribbons for my hair, which Antonio artfully arranged. For the rest of the morning I had to be careful about moving my head so that the velvet and satin and grosgrain would stay in place.

Will called a couple of times. He was staying with his friend Benni, a few blocks away. I think his phone calls were just nervous check-ins, reassuring himself that all was well, that we were going forward. We'd had an argument the night before because he wanted to stay with me and was forbidden to do so by my cousin. After much loud discussion, we dismissed him, and he never again climbed the marble stairs to my apartment door, yellow rose in hand, love all over his beaming face.

Mary and I finished up my final packing and left everything I was taking with me on our honeymoon in the living room so that Dorothy, my superbly competent assistant, and her husband, Raymond, could gather up my valises and pack them in the Beetle after the ceremony. Mary and I then walked with my wedding garments to Faith's apartment. Her doorman greeted me with a huge grin and we were whisked up to the third floor. Faith's bedroom was designated as my dressing room.

To my shock, when we arrived at the apartment, my mother- and father-in-law-to-be were already there. We never expected them to be at the ceremony because the church would condemn them of mortal sin for being present, but there they were, along with Will's brother and sister-in-law. The two women were delighted to be in the midst of my getting ready. I was not as delighted. Finding their comments and chatter distracting and unnerving, I didn't know how to ask them to leave the room. My cousin did. Noticing my increasing distress, she cleared the bedroom, asking everyone to wait outside. Mary's manner may not have been the most gentle, but her results were always effective. Aunt Ceal had joined us in the bedroom by this point, so I had the support of two women of my family. But, Mother was not there.

The first of several challenges to the plan of the day occurred. Lyn, the best man, called me to say he couldn't make it. No one asked any questions. We all knew he felt too concerned to be seen in public with my cousin. Will wasn't aware of Lyn's call because he hadn't yet arrived at the site. He would have to ask one of our guests to step in as his best man when he arrived at 11:30. The judge was to arrive just before noon and the ceremony would take place exactly at noon.

Guests began arriving around 11:45, and Will was still not in sight. While our friends were sipping Champagne, I was pacing in the bedroom, wondering where my always prompt husband-to-be could be. I felt like a prisoner in the bedroom, unable to communicate with anyone except my cousin and my aunt. It never occurred to me to try to reach Will by telephone.

My dear sister Ann arrived from California and we had great tears and hugs together. She had defied Mother and Dad, and although she knew that any Catholic witnessing our union would be committing sin according to church rules of the day, she came to be with us.

Time was now becoming an issue. By 11:55, neither Will nor the judge had arrived. Will finally appeared around 12:15, somehow unaware that he was late.

To this day still compulsive about promptness, he doesn't know why he was late for his wedding. Told that his best man wasn't coming, Will turned to his oft-estranged brother and asked him to step in. Richard graciously did so.

At 12:30, Judge Amos Basil appeared, apologetic that a court matter had delayed him. It was a Wednesday, after all! Now we could begin.

I was still hidden in the bedroom but knew that Aunt Ceal and Uncle Wes were in charge outside. With Will's instructions, the judge announced that he was about to begin and that anyone who did not want to witness our vows could step into the hallway until the ceremony was complete. No one moved. Not my in-laws, not the priests who dared to be with us, not the nun and brother who were there, not any of our Catholic friends and family. All stayed to witness our marriage and to cheer when the vows were complete. Alleluias indeed! What joy, what praise, what love in that beautiful place.

Will and I agreed to love and honor for richer, for poorer, in sickness and in health, forsaking all others until death do us part. Judge Basil led us through it all, sweetly and firmly guiding us through the "I do" and "I will," comforting us through the moments of "Oh my gosh, this is a big decision." We made no commitments to be faithful members of a congregation. We committed to sharing a life and the values dear to us that had brought us to this seemingly impossible day.

I cried through it all. It was only years later that I understood that I was both joyful and sorrowful on the most important day of my life. I was grieving the estrangement from my parents, I was emotionally exhausted from all the snares and challenges of getting to this day, and I was fearful about a journey without road marks. Most importantly, I was so happy to be with this man whom I admired and adored. I couldn't bear to leave his side as we mingled with our guests, afraid it was all a dream that couldn't possibly have happened.

After the Champagne toast, we dined on a luscious variety of French sandwiches that were nestled in large carved-out brioche, served by the two French butlers. And, with minimum ceremony, when Uncle Wes made an announcement, we cut our beautifully tiered orange cake. Years later, Will complained that he never had a bite of it. I don't remember tasting any of the food. I do remember the tears of happiness and sadness and of being so thrilled at seeing our guests that I would say, "I didn't know you were coming!" to each, as if I hadn't invited them.

No professional photographers, no wedding planner, no organ nor string quartet were in that room. Dear and courageous friends and four family members for each of us, blessings galore, laughter and tears flowing. It was a Great Alleluia Day!

Our guests had all departed by three in the afternoon, except for Dorothy and Raymond. They helped us pile our gifts and suitcases into the car, slogging through the snow piled up at the curb in front of Faith's apartment. We chugged away in Will's Beetle that was packed to the roof with some clothing and wedding gifts. I was leaving my home and my beloved city. I didn't even think about it.

Our first stop on our shortened honeymoon was Mount Sinai Hospital, where I threw my bouquet to Faith in her hospital bed and we spent time with her, telling her as many details of the day as we could remember. We then drove on to our three-day honeymoon at Stonehenge, a luxurious inn in Ridgefield, Connecticut. We had decided to cancel an island trip since Will had limited vacation time from the university.

That evening, around 7 o'clock, we pulled up to one of the beautiful cottages at the inn. Dr. and Mrs. Scanlan entered the cottage. The living room was lit by the blaze from a huge stone fireplace. A bouquet of yellow roses shone on the low table in front of the fire, compliments of "The Roses Man." Our most elegant dinner was about to be served with the first bottle from the special case of Margaux wine we had purchased to begin our uncharted life together. And so it began.

SCANDAL

A Catholic Wedding

After Words

Married life in Binghamton was heavenly. We were luxuriating in the afterglow of tackling the enormous social, cultural and ecclesiastical obstacles we had faced, now out of the fray, living in the country outside of Binghamton, on a new adventure.

I was a happy homemaker but frustrated at first in my attempts to find any professional work the least bit similar to the magazine. About three months after we arrived in this new land, I walked in to my new job. There were no magazines, but I had found a plum public relations position. "We're in the best spots in town," Will remarked. "Me at the university, you at the arts center." We certainly were in the center of the intellectual and cultural life of the area, small comfort from our sorrow at leaving Manhattan.

We had made every effort to keep Will's previous life under wraps in our present world. In 1968, a resigned priest was unusual. We wanted to be accepted on equal terms with new friends, colleagues and neighbors, and not be the subject of gossip and speculation. We thought we had outwitted the gossips.

As I entered the administrative offices of the Roberson Center for the Arts and Sciences, an organization that housed a museum, art gallery, planetarium, historical society, opera company and dance company, that first day on the new job, I heard the head secretary say to everyone around her, "Here's the girl from New York who's married to the priest." Amidst the clacking and giggling, not a comfortable entrance. I did manage to gather the strength and later asked her to be more sensitive in the future.

It was never comfortable, however, to be the object of everyone's curiosity at a faculty dinner party. It became a joke between us. I was Jezebel or Will was the fallen priest, or he was the dirty old man and I was the unsuspecting innocent. Each encounter differed, depending on the source. As we began to expect curiosity, we could laugh more about people's perceptions and expectations.

We could not laugh, however, at the continued shunning by my parents. When my health was affected and I developed physical problems in response to their silence and condemnation, Will became angry at them, especially at my mother. At one point, he wrote her a letter, more like a sermon, chastising her for what he called her cruelty to me and quoting scripture to remind her about charity. He ended it:

I do not ask that you be dishonest to yourself, rather the contrary. I do ask that you take a wider view of what you are doing. Some of the members of the family suggest that you regret your untenable position but are unable to find a way out of it. The way out, I state firmly, is clear and obvious.

In conclusion, I wish to inform you that I have petitioned formally for a dispensation. I have no information as to the outcome of my petition as yet. I have reason to believe it shall be granted shortly. Whether it is or not, I believe your brutal course of action serves no positive purpose. For your own welfare, you two must find a way out of your impasse. I assure you of my willingness to do what I can to assist you.

She never responded.

Since my pain was not going away, we decided, after long and careful discussion that we would begin the process to bring us all some peace. Will had been granted a leave of absence from his assignment in the priesthood and had not functioned as a priest since August 1967 when he left for Binghamton. On the same day in November that we became engaged, he had requested a leave of absence from his priestly obligations. It was only after our wedding the following January 1968 that he received an answer to that letter to his bishop.

Being married in the Catholic Church didn't mean anything to us. Marriage vows, we agreed, were between two people and didn't really need religious imprimatur. Since dispensations from the Vatican were slow and uncertain, we didn't vigorously pursue the archaic Roman Catholic process. In the notorious grayness of Binghamton that winter, we realized that my parents might be reconciled to our marriage only if we were married "properly" in the Catholic Church.

"We don't care about this," Will said to me. "But if we get the Vatican documentation, and then get married in the church, your parents will come around." I agreed that being married in the church wasn't at all important to me. But I also agreed the shunning by my parents was more painful than I had imagined.

The "proper way" of laicization for a priest, usually referred to in blaring media headlines as "defrocking a priest" starts with a priest requesting dispensation from his clerical obligations from his bishop and then from the Vatican. Once the mysterious process is completed, the priest is released from those obligations and receives no clerical benefits. The church is no longer required to feed and house a laicized priest, and he is no longer legally allowed to perform sacramental duties such as distributing Communion, hearing confessions, marrying or administering the last rites at death.

However, there is a belief that ordination to the Catholic priesthood leaves an indelible mark on the soul. A resigned priest can validly use his sacramental powers in an appropriate situation, such as an imminent death. To say Mass or administer any of the other sacraments would be technically illicit. But common thinking persisted, "Once a priest, always a priest."

To be dispensed by the Vatican from his priestly vows Will had to undergo a canonical trial. He had requested a dispensation so that we could have a Catholic marriage ceremony in a church. We decided to do this, thinking it would give us an avenue of reconciliation with my family. We figured that once we had taken all the complicated ecclesiastical steps necessary and received the sacrament of matrimony, I would be back in everyone's good graces. We were doing this for other people, not ourselves. And we were doing it for my health.

We wanted none of the blaring headlines. That was an important reason we had left New York City. Will's position in the Brooklyn Diocese was perfect for a media scandal.

And so, he wrote to his bishop:

I seek laicization because I no longer feel that I can do the work of a priest because of the serious and prolonged questions that have arisen in my mind about: a) the efficacy of the pastoral ministry as presently exercised; b) the necessity and value of celibacy for the priest; and c) the importance of the marriage relationship. These questions have so diluted my unity of purpose, that I am not able to function as a priest.

He continued:

My life as a priest was most usual. I was an assistant pastor in a small parish in Queens County for 4½ years. After that time, I was appointed assistant superintendent of schools. I remained in this office for nine years. During this nine-year period, I acquired a master's degree in educational psychology and a doctorate in educational administration and supervision.

During my ministry, I regularly and sincerely performed all the required and recommend pious and penitential works. I said Mass daily for more than 10 years. I read the breviary regularly with as much devotion as possible. I made daily mental prayer for 13 years, daily holy hour for more than 10, and thereafter did so several times each week. I pursued ecclesiastical study as my work allowed, in areas judged important to the ministry. I made an annual retreat, and frequent monthly days of recollection. I had a confessor for 13 years. I always spent my vacations with my fellow priests. I exercised the ministry to the best of my ability and according to the best available norms. My conscience is quite clear.

My decision to resign from the active ministry and to marry was made in several stages. In 1963, I had serious questions about the efficacy and relevance of the ministry as exercised. Those questions have persisted. I had come to question a great deal about the institutions of the Church and many of the ascetical theories and practices which form the basis for clerical life. In 1965, I knew I no longer wished to continue in the clerical life In 1966, I began to questions the value of the celibate state as a necessary concomitant to the priestly life, and as a state superior, in itself, to the married state.

I prayed and thought a great deal about all these questions. I discussed them with my confessor and with other priests. I sought and received medical advice as to my ability to make a proper decision. In my retreat in 1967, I discussed the matter of my resigning from the priesthood, in frank and forthright terms, with a religious priest, and then decided to resign and to consider the married state. I received a leave of absence from my ordinary. Within a short period of time, my resignation from the clerical state and marriage seemed, to me, to be my most honest and honorable path. In good conscience, I now request a dispensation to pursue what I have judged to be the correct course of my life …

… I have been considering such a move for more than two years, and am not making my request in anger or unhappiness. My priestly and professional associates are of the highest caliber. I am not protesting, beginning a movement or making a dramatic gesture. On the contrary, I want to clarify my thinking by adopting a different perspective. My work as a diocesan official and a secular priest requires great dedication. Such dedication, in its turn, demands

a clear vision of the required tasks and their inter-relationships. My vision has become unclear.

Early that summer of 1968, after receiving his request for dispensation, Will received a call from the Tribunal of the Diocese of Brooklyn to appear at the chancery office for a canonical trial. The years with Dr. Sullivan were to be the most important evidence of the trial.

"I always knew," Will triumphantly shouted, "that having Joe Sullivan as my psychiatrist would be my trump card with the church!" Not only was Sullivan in a prominent position in the Archdiocese of New York, he was also a Catholic professional, having plenty of weight with church officials because of that affiliation.

The trial would be the penultimate step in the application submitted to the Vatican through the Brooklyn bishop. Then there would be a request from that office to dispense Will. He would be "reduced to the lay state."

Will had entered the clerical state when he was in seminary. Before his ordination to the priesthood, he and his classmates had been ordained to the orders of lector, porter, exorcist and acolyte during the third year of seminary, followed by the major orders of sub-deacon, deacon and priest in the fifth and sixth year. Once dispensed, these sacraments of holy orders would no longer be valid.

Will was asked to come alone for his trial. He gathered all the requested documents and went off to Brooklyn eagerly. He was excited. I was a nervous wreck. I had too many movies of medieval horrors in my mind, imagining an Inquisition tribunal of wicked men torturing my beloved. In fact, there was only one member from the Tribunal present, who taped Will's testimony about his life as a priest and his decision to resign his priesthood. The judge showed Will the testimony he had received from Dr. Sullivan, certifying that he was emotionally unable to remain an active priest.

Will and Dr. Sullivan knew the most acceptable reason for granting dispensations.

Therefore when Will contacted him, two years after we were married, he agreed to disclose information about his patient to the tribunal. He confirmed in his testimony that Father Scanlan was not psychologically able to be celibate and, therefore, could not, by the church's very own rules, continue to function as a Roman Catholic priest. It was his gift to Will.

There were other testimonies as well and, after little more than an hour, Will was dismissed and told to wait to hear the results. He never received a transcript of the proceeding and never requested one. As I protested vigorously about our rights and our need to see the documents, Will quietly and firmly reminded me that "it doesn't matter. It's not real." The only "real" ground for dispensation at that time was that a priest was incapable of being celibate. The only promises a priest makes at ordination are celibacy and obedience to his bishop.

He returned home late that night recounted the "trial" with humor and assured me he wasn't harmed, that it was just part of the process, that all that we wanted would take place. "You know, Mary," he said, "these guys know what's going on. I feel sorry for them. Like Hugh said, they have miserable, lonely lives. We're going to be fine."

On July 6, 1968; Will received a letter from the Tribunal of the Diocese of Brooklyn signed by the chancellor, Monsignor Joseph King, stating: "I can't give you any exact idea of how long your case will take. I would say that normally it would take about two or three months, but Rome works on a skeleton force, rumor has it, during August and the first two weeks in September, or thereabouts. That might delay it a bit … I know you are anxious about it, but I'm sure it will work out all right."

Eight months later, in March 1969, Will received a telegram from the chancellor, saying simply, "Roman document arrived. Call me." The deed was done. He was dispensed, defrocked, laicized. We never saw an official document from the Vatican, nor did we ever ask for one.

Shortly after the official word was received, we were given permission to be married by a Catholic priest. Someone from the bishop's office in the Diocese of Syracuse called to say we were all cleared for a Catholic marriage and gave us the name of a local priest to contact, which we did.

We did receive a letter from my parents, which read:

Dear Mary,

Your letter was most welcome, and made us happy and thankful. I sure you're both relieved that these problems have been solved.

Naturally you have never been out of our thoughts or prayers. You have always been regarded as one of our daughters, with love. We are glad to hear of your deep love for each other. From our own experience, we know you can face anything when you have this love.

On another gray and rainy Sunday afternoon in March 1969, we met the priest in Vestal, New York who had been assigned by some church official to marry us. At the rectory door, a nervous housekeeper showed us into the parlor. The priest appeared within a few minutes, announcing, "I've never done one of these before!" and pulled down the shades in the room. When we gently asked him why he was doing that, he told us he was performing a secret ceremony. "There can be no witnesses," he replied emphatically, "and I need to be sure no one is watching."

He then closed the door to the gloomy room and asked us to stand in front of him in a makeshift ceremonial setting. Noticing that we were wearing wedding bands, he asked us to remove them so that he could bless them in the traditional Catholic wedding ceremony. I giggled internally as I tried unsuccessfully to pull my wide band over my enlarged knuckle "Can't seem to get it off, Father," I said. Will just ignored the request. At the poor man's prompting, we repeated our vows and he gave us his blessing, stuttering with nerves through the brief ritual. "How about a glass of sherry?" he asked when we completed our vows. We demurred and swiftly escaped the rectory. It was now a raw late winter afternoon. Most people in Vestal were probably tucked in their homes, reading newspapers, getting ready for the week, catching up on schoolwork for the next day. Alone in our victory over the institutional demands, we drove away from the Victorian church relic towards the newest restaurant in town across from the university campus to celebrate the joy of my pregnancy and the promise of new life.

The following week, we wrote a letter to our parents, telling them that we were married in the church and expecting a child. A few weeks later we agreed to meet my parents for lunch in New York City. We never discussed the source of our estrangement. We just talked.

Acknowledgments

Marion Roach Smith, author, teacher, colleague and friend, urged me – no bugged me – to start writing my memoir. Without her support and persistence, *A Will of Her Own* would not have come into being, and I am grateful.

Thanks to Rob Brill for his professional editing support. He brought great experience, questions, skill and interest. This work would have been very different without his guidance.

I am grateful for my dear friends, Reverend Starr Regan DiCiurcio, Ellen Sadowski, and Mary Valentis who graciously offered me their talents and exceptional intelligence, making grand suggestions and improving my work.

The writing group of Mary Kate McCarty, Al Stumph and William Swire and I came together to encourage each other, to nudge and sometimes threaten each other towards completion. I thank them for their patience and honesty over the years.

A circle of writing friends inspired new ideas, and offered wonderful criticism when needed – always. Anne Mulderry, Cheryl Gorn, Regina Kalet, and the late Dick Berkson were faithful colleagues. I thank them.

Lorayne Ruthman never stopped being interested, bringing her expert technical skills to this work. I literally could not have done this without her.

There are members of my family whom I asked to shared this journey with me and gave me loving support. I thank them.

I also thank Debbi Wraga of ShiresPress Publishing at Northshire Bookstore for her publishing expertise, her calm and reassuring assistance, for her integrity and her sense of humor.

Over the years, Will patiently and lovingly encouraged me. Many a night he listened, for the umpteenth time, while I read him a chapter and asked his opinion. He always gave it! He shared so much information about his life before me, did the research when necessary, and never complained. I'm hoping that he's pleased with the results of our work. I can just hear him saying, " Atta girl, Mare."

ABOUT THE AUTHOR
Mary Scanlan

Prior to founding Scanlan Communications Group, Mary Scanlan was as an editor at *Harper's Bazaar* and on the editorial staff of the national professional journals for The Institute of Electrical and Electronic Engineers (IEEE).

Mary Scanlan earned a bachelor of arts in English from Queens College and a master's in education from Russell Sage College. Her writings have appeared in The Penman Review and Existere, and broadcast on the Capital Region National Public Radio affiliate.

She lives in Glenmont, New York.

CPSIA information can be obtained
at www.ICGtesting.com
Printed in the USA
LVOW01s1911120216

474589LV00024B/120/P